Disrupted Schooling

Schooling

the growth of the special unit

edited by

Mel Lloyd-Smith MA MEd

Lecturer in Education, University of Warwick

Pg 55.

John Murray

© M. Lloyd-Smith 1984

First published 1984
by John Murray (Publishers) Ltd
50 Albemarle Street, London W1X 4BD

Typeset in Great Britain by
Fakenham Photosetting Ltd,
Fakenham, Norfolk.
Printed and bound in Great Britain at
The Pitman Press, Bath.

British Library Cataloguing in Publication Data

  Disrupted Schooling
  1. Problem children – Education
  I. Lloyd-Smith, Mel
  371.8'1   LC4801

ISBN 0–7195–4000–3

Contents

Acknowledgements

I would like to thank Chris Brown for the perceptive and constructive comments he made on the penultimate draft of this collection and Ann Cochrane at John Murray, not only for her discernment and efficiency but also for her patience and encouragement. A number of people have been involved in typing and retyping; particular thanks are due to Alison Negus and Jean Selvey.

Several of the contributors make use of material collected from empirical studies of special units and we wish to acknowledge the help which made these various studies possible. Particularly we thank those teachers and pupils who generously tolerated our intrusion into their affairs.

M L-S

Notes on the contributors

Cathy Bird is currently conducting research into the police and the community at the Police Foundation in London. She was formerly Research Fellow at the Educational Studies Unit at Brunel University and was co-author of *Disaffected Pupils* published in 1980.

David Coulby is a lecturer in the Comparative Education Department at the London University Institute of Education. Prior to this he taught for nine years, mainly in east London. He was in charge of the ILEA Division 5 Support Team working within mainstream schools with pupils identified as being disruptive.

Terry Emerson is teacher in charge of the North Camden Support Unit which serves five north London comprehensive schools. In his previous post at a mixed comprehensive school in Wembley between 1977 and 1979, he was responsible for setting up and running an off-site unit.

Mike Golby is a senior lecturer in education at the University of Exeter. He was a primary school teacher and deputy head before becoming a college of education lecturer and then a member of the central academic staff at the Open University, where he was a member of the teams responsible for the Curriculum Design and Development Course and the Urban Education Course. He is currently the European Editor of the *Journal of Curriculum Studies*.

John Leavold is headmaster of Acton High School, having formerly been head of Elthorne High School and deputy head of Twyford High School, all in the London Borough of Ealing. His previous career encompassed technical, grammar and comprehensive schools, teaching physical education and social studies.

Mel Lloyd-Smith is a lecturer at the University of Warwick where he has responsibility for the in-service courses in special educational needs. He worked as a teacher in secondary schools and in the prison service for ten years before going into teacher training. He has published several articles on teacher training and special education.

John McDermott   is headmaster of George Salter High School in Sandwell. He has taught in comprehensive schools since 1975 in Manchester, Stockport and Chesterfield. Two of these schools had special units, and as senior master and deputy head he was closely involved in their work.

Geoff Whitty   is Lecturer in Education and co-ordinator of the Urban Education Programme at King's College, London. Previously he taught in two comprehensive schools and at the University of Bath. He has published widely in the areas of the sociology of education and social studies teaching.

1

Introduction: The growth of special units for disaffected pupils

Mel Lloyd-Smith

A prominent educational development during the 1970s was the adoption of special units or classes as a strategy for dealing with pupils whose behaviour was creating serious control problems for teachers. The evolution of this policy, whilst being unsystematic, was both widespread and rapid, and by the end of the decade special units had become a commonplace feature of provision in most local education authorities. It was never entirely clear, however, whether this represented a response to a new problem or a new method of dealing with an old one. The popular belief was that disruption in schools was no longer a comparatively isolated phenomenon but a new and ubiquitous malaise of our times, reflecting a general decline in behavioural standards. The establishment of special units, therefore, seems to have been a development forced upon the school system.

This was not, however, a discrete development but one which was linked historically and conceptually with two notable contemporary trends. The first was that represented in the deschooling movement which in its pure form called for the disestablishment of all schools but which in practice inspired some critics of the existing systems to create alternative or 'free' schools. These were generally small and, because this was the only market available for such enterprises, aimed specifically at meeting the needs of pupils in a particular locality who found it difficult to accept or be accepted by conventional schools. Often their curricula represented radical departures from traditional models and though literacy and numeracy usually provided the core, much of the remaining curriculum was typically neighbourhood based. Although the establishment and professional bodies expressed some disquiet at such developments – the NUT, for example, called teachers in free schools 'educational quislings' (see Head 1974) – they were tolerated because they provided what was often the only alternative for pupils who appeared to have opted out of the state education system.

The second trend which can be seen as an important part of the background to the rise of special units, is that embodied in the so-called 'Great Debate', the widespread public discussion of educational standards. This has concentrated particularly on the relevance of current education to the nation's commercial and industrial needs, as in James Callaghan's widely reported speech at Ruskin College in 1976, but has also strongly called into question the quality of present-day education. Allegations were frequently made that children today are achieving less than previous generations, particularly in the basic areas of the curriculum. Permeating the 'Great Debate' has been an economic ideology of education which justifies greater bureaucratic intervention on the grounds of greater accountability to the economy. In his highly publicised speech at the North of England Conference early in 1984, the Secretary of State for Education, Sir Keith Joseph, set out his proposals for the improvement of educational standards through increased central control over the curriculum and the examination system. At the same time he made it clear that he regarded the behaviour of pupils to be an important component of standards in schools. This last aspect of the speech reflects the view which had increasingly been asserted in the popular press that teachers have been losing the ability to discipline their pupils, to exert the traditional controls aimed at instilling obedience, good manners and acceptance of the work ethic.

Superficially, there would seem to be some logical continuity between the problem thus defined and the emergence of special units in large numbers during the 1970s. Units could be depicted as necessary emergency measures designed to relieve teachers of the more unreasonably difficult pupils so that they were able to carry out their primary obligation to the nation. However, notions reflecting the alternative schooling thesis are also apparent in common justifications of special units. Here the purpose is seen as rescuing pupils from oppressive institutions into which they cannot comfortably fit and providing them with a special form of education or treatment.

The nature of this required treatment is open to a variety of interpretations and the titles given to special units portray a wide range of different intentions (see Topping and Quelch 1976; Golby 1979; ACE 1980). For example, 'exclusion centres' and 'adjustment groups' would seem to have primarily a disciplinary purpose while the titles of 'guidance', 'diagnostic' and 'assessment' units imply a clinical role. In some situations the units provide sanctuary and are so named, in others they provide what is first and foremost an education programme and are identified by terms such as 'tutorial centre', 'individual work unit' and 'tuition unit'.

The first systematic national survey (DES, 1978) showed that in 1977 there were 239 units in sixty-nine local authorities, over 80 per cent of them having been established since 1973. Almost four thousand places were available in the units, the majority being for children of secondary school age though forty-six units took primary children also, while a further twenty-one served primary schools only. Only three years later, the ACE Survey (1980) revealed that the number of units had risen by a hundred and they collectively provided places for 6,791 pupils. The Inner London Education Authority had by then developed its units provision to the extent of supporting 226 units containing a total of 3,800 pupils. As has been pointed out before (Lloyd-Smith 1979; Young *et al.* 1980) a new and significant sector of special provision and a new category of child came into being in the last decade, notwithstanding the fact that during the same period special schools for maladjusted pupils were expanding their numbers also.

Numbers of maladjusted pupils

(These figures include boys and girls receiving part-time and full-time special education in maintained and non-maintained schools; they also include those awaiting admission.

1970	13,360	1976	19,938
1972	16,030	1978	21,071
1974	17,547	1980	21,106

Sources: 1970–1979 DES *Statistics of Education*, Vol. 1;
            1980 DES *Statistics of Schools*.

As the new field of education manifested in the growth of units was being first cultivated and accounts of the early initiatives began to appear, diverse and sometimes contradictory features were repeatedly arising, not only regarding treatment methods but also with respect to basic rationales and the identification of aims. A somewhat muddled picture was emerging, and the fundamental reason why such a development should have seemed necessary remained likewise unclear.

How then is this trend to be interpreted? At one level it simply represents the evolution of a policy which increasingly emphasises the removal of problem pupils from the classroom and the appointment of specially designated teachers to deal with them. But further important questions remain. For instance, is it the case that problem behaviour is increasing in quantity and degree to the extent of now being beyond the control of the ordinary class teacher? Or could it be that the boundaries of acceptable behaviour are shifting? Are schools undergoing changes which make the problems more acute?

By far the most commonly held view was that there was an increase in the number of children showing themselves unwilling or unable to conform to traditionally accepted standards of behaviour; that is, that contemporary society had produced a generation of pupils among whom a greater proportion behaved in a deviant way.

The report on the DES survey clearly accepted this interpretation and, summarising the views of administrators, psychologists, heads and teachers who were interviewed, accounted for it in two ways. The first explanation was in terms of a general social decline indicated by such phenomena as 'family breakdown, lack of respect for authority, a fall in moral standards and a widespread lack of discipline' (p. 41). The second explanation referred to changes in schools, their size, organisation and curriculum, which made them less able to cope with deviance than in former times, The 'external' theory of causes was vividly represented in a report by the Liverpool Education Committee (1974), *The Suspended Child*, which expressed the conviction that society and culture were breaking down because of 'the prevailing climate of permissiveness ... and the move of the courts away from deterrents to care and therapy'. The factors underlying disruptive behaviour in schools were seen here as social and material deprivation, broken homes and 'parental irresponsibility'.

The Pack Report on truancy and indiscipline in schools in Scotland (Scottish Education Department 1977) expressed doubt about the schools' ability to deal adequately with problems associated with current social trends. The main sources of conflict arise from permissive values in society, the media – especially television – and the influence of parents who expect schools to enforce standards of behaviour for their children which they themselves do not support. Similar clusters of factors are identified in the reports of the Cumbria Education Department (1976) and the Staffordshire Education Committee (1977).

Teachers' professional associations have regularly drawn attention to the apparently growing problem of disruptive behaviour and have also offered explanations. The Association of Headmistresses (1973), in a pamphlet which sets out the schools' obligation to ensure the 'adjustment' of its pupils, identified 'over-indulgence in the early years' as a cause of later disruptive behaviour (presumably the major cause as no other specific factors are mentioned). The National Association of Schoolmasters (1974) unequivocally proclaimed that the growth of indiscipline had its origins in 'society' in which there had been a 'reaction against military and economic disciplines of the war years'. Other baleful influences were certain theories of child psychology and the teacher training establishments which have been steadily inculcating 'poor attitudes' in new entrants to the profession. The Professional Association of Teachers (1976), reporting on its survey of discipline problems of all kinds, concluded that parental attitudes were the major causal factor, the second most important factor being class size. Broader societal causes were identified by the National Union of Teachers (1976) in its document on discipline, but rather than seeing these in the form of attitudes or values which encourage disruptive behaviour, the authors saw the origins as partly being due to social deprivation. They argued that disruptive behaviour is often associated with emotional instability; this is in turn associated with academic failure which is associated with lack of parental interest, low literacy levels in the home and the poor material conditions which signify social deprivation. The overall emphasis in the NUT discussion, however, (and a feature which distinguishes it from the others) was on a large range of factors internal to the education system. In particular, authors of the pamphlet cited policy decisions which have led to over-large classes generally, inadequate levels of staff to work with low achievers and insufficient funds to replace old and inadequate buildings. At the individual school level, a number of organisational and curriculum aspects of current policy were alleged to exacerbate problems of discipline and control. The National Association of Headteachers also entered the debate, going as far as to demand the establishment of special institutions for disruptive pupils. These 'coolers', as the Association referred to them (*The Times Educational Supplement*, October 1978), would perform the function of 'rehabilitating' the unruly pupils and making them fit for return to 'normal' classes.

These and similar declarations all tend to oversimplify and even mythologise the complex question of causation. They seldom offer evidence, though in some cases extrapolations have been made from studies which attempt to explain problems related to disruption, such as truancy and delinquency. What they seem to represent is a generalised, popular belief, one which is frequently voiced in the popular press and on television and accepted and freely used by those who are critical of or depressed by changes in contemporary society. These statements also, in some instances, carry an obvious ideological loading. The teachers' associations, for instance, in their pronouncements seek to deny that teachers themselves are responsible for low standards of behaviour in schools, and they sometimes use the problem as a means to other ends, in appeals for the reduction of class sizes, for example.

The 'changing social values' thesis, however, does have some validity. Societies which have in recent years increasingly stressed values relating to individual liberty may create conflict for young people who are still compelled by law to attend school. On a more general level, the notions underlying the 'cultural divergence' theories of educational failure among working class children may well apply in the case of disruptive pupil behaviour. It may well be the case that some unco-operative or disruptive behaviour arises from strain between certain values embedded in the education system and its methods of operation, and other oppositional values which children and their parents absorb from the constellation of changing social values. To what extent this perspective can in itself provide an adequate explanation remains an open question.

Professional associations occupying other vantage points perceive the problem in a different way. The British Association of Social Workers, in a document on excluded children (1977), accuses teachers of being too eager to 'ditch the trouble makers'. It argues that

Children are too easily branded as truants or are suspended from schools because of difficulties faced by the children in school: rarely will the school ever admit that its handling of the child might have contributed to the child's behaviour.

Such a perspective directs attention away from the social values variable to factors within the education system and within the value systems of the teaching profession. It allows one to pose the question: could any increase in disruptive behaviour be due to the shifting of behavioural boundaries within educational contexts? Apparently none of the commentators mentioned so far has considered this possibility. It is theoretically possible, however, that the increase in behaviour problems could partly be due to a reduced willingness among teachers to tolerate 'bad' behaviour. A number of educational trends in recent years could be seen as providing a basis for such shifts within the professional ideologies of teachers. Some improvements in conditions have recently been achieved in the increased use, for example, of more teacher aides to carry out menial non-teaching tasks such as meal supervision. There has also been an improvement, at secondary school level, in the provision of other supportive services – in secretarial and administrative teams as well as in the resources area. Alongside these developments there has been a tendency to make the school's responsibility for dealing with its pupils' personal and social problems more explicit. The welfare of socially deprived children has become much more an educational issue, and the responses of social service agencies have increasingly become based on the school or have at least involved fuller collaboration with schools. In the past two decades attempts to establish a 'teacher as social worker' role have occasionally been made. Craft (1966 and 1967), for example, has argued that teachers can accept a welfare role, though a limited one confined to identifying and referring children with problems, while Musgrave (1975) stresses a welfare role for teachers in relation to the pupil's home. Different general approaches to such responsibility have also been discussed as in Rose and Marshall (1974) where an 'integrative' approach, emphasising the overall development of the child, is contrasted with the traditional 'instrumental' approach.

Rather than effecting a redefinition of the general teacher role, however, this increased interest in the needs of children with problems or with non-normal educational career patterns has led to the creation of new structures and specialist personnel within traditional education organisations, notably the establishment of specific counselling or pastoral care systems. One possible consequence of this is that it is now easier for ordinary class teachers to say that the pupil with problems (or the problem pupil) is no longer their concern but is the responsibility of specialist staff, paid and in some cases trained to deal with such pupils. In such a situation, a class teacher is able to regard certain behaviours as requiring specialist treatment simply because the treatment is now available. Therefore it is possible, as it were, to 'draw in' the boundary between acceptable and unacceptable behaviour in the classroom.

Such changes in professional ideologies occur within a general theoretical context relating to deviance and conformity. There have been definite tendencies to regard forms of deviant behaviour in children as internal problems of the individual child or as emanating from 'unsatisfactory' home backgrounds. A teacher's professional ideologies will reflect these dominant theoretical orientations, which in the main focus upon the individual child and aspects of his or her early socialisation and to a much lesser extent on the arenas within which the problem behaviour occurs.

A valuable insight into teachers' perspectives is found in the study by Richardson (1983) which includes a detailed examination of documents, reports and conference proceedings, dealing with problem behaviour in schools, which emanated from government departments and major teacher unions during the period 1939–1980. He shows how the notion of 'the difficult child' gradually became transformed and reified. This occurred as theories of causation were developed in which 'indiscipline' was increasingly conflated with concepts such as maladjustment and delinquency. Through this process the reified 'type' of problem pupil became incorporated into an increasingly complex network of structures and procedures for ascertainment, referral, treatment and segregation. Richardson suggests that although this debate was conducted in the rhetoric of humanitarianism and care, it was covertly a justification for ridding schools of pupils whose presence was seen by the teaching profession and policy makers as threatening the educational status quo and the power of teachers.

Only relatively recently have studies begun to suggest the importance of institutional processes involved in schooling for an understanding of children's behaviour. The work of Hargreaves *et al.* (1975); Reynolds (1976a and 1976b); Reynolds and Murgatroyd (1977); and Rutter *et al.* (1979) provides strong evidence to support the view that in order to understand fully deviant behaviour among school pupils, the situational contexts within which the behaviour occurs must be taken into account. The structures and processes which characterise these contexts are as important in any analysis as factors relating to individual characteristics of pupils or their family background.

One aspect which seldom features in studies of school behaviour is the economic context within which schooling exists. The functions of education have been analysed in political economic terms at a conceptual level revealing, in the work of Bowles and Gintis (1976) for instance, the way that education systems reproduce social relationships and features reflecting authority and control required to maintain a particular mode of production. However, as yet there has been very little work done on this at the empirical level (though see Willis 1977; Reeves 1977 and 1978; Corrigan 1979). One issue which would seem to have crucial importance on any examination of the apparent increase in disruptive behaviour in the UK in the 1970s, is the impact of the economic crisis in this period. The prospect of unemployment which faced more and more older school children in these years could, it might be hypothesised, have had a direct effect on their attitudes to schooling and their responses to authority and control in school. The promise of better jobs and higher incomes can no longer be credibly held out by teachers as rewards for conformity to school behavioural standards and acceptance of the work ethic.

Although the importance of the situational contexts of school behaviour and the economic context of schooling in general is becoming increasingly recognised in the literature, it is suggested here that the dominant teacher perspectives on 'bad' behaviour remain those which derive from individual or family-based pathological explanations. Theoretical perspectives and action alike are underpinned by the ubiquitous 'medical model' which has often been a taken-for-granted framework uncritically applied to social problems. This can have the effect of diverting attention away from the real causes of a problem and emphasising means of controlling or suppressing the symptoms. At the same time it can have the effect of amplifying the original problem in a self-fulfilling social process. One form of this can be seen in the extreme case of the ostensible rise in the incidence of 'hyperactivity' among school children in the USA (see Box 1977; Schrag and Divoky 1981).

It will be apparent from the foregoing discussion that no clear-cut answer can be expected to the question: what does the recent proliferation of special 'disruptive' units mean? It will be clear, furthermore, that an answer in terms of, say, weakening self-control among the young in a society whose behavioural standards are in decline, is inadequate; it is naîvely one-dimensional, neglecting several fundamental variables. Shifts among general social factors may well be relevant but equally so are changes in economic conditions and in policies relating to the organisation of schools and the design of curricula. As indicated earlier, it is also felt that an examination of changing professional ideologies among teachers could provide a useful perspective on the phenomenon. From this point of view special units are objectifications of certain beliefs about children, about 'proper' behaviour, deviance and the rightful duties of teachers, beliefs which through the subtle processes of negotiation become 'legitimising categories' and serve to define (in this case) those behaviours which call for separate specialist treatment, and thereby 'create' a category of pupils.

A stance which attempts to take account of these factors invokes an interpretation which depicts the phenomenon (the sudden proliferation of 'disruptive units') as socially created, the result of social processes operating at various levels within the education system itself. As indicated earlier, this view does not deny the influences of external societal factors. Indeed, this perspective, whilst seeking to expose and analyse those internal processes which tend to remain hidden, also attempts to comprehend the broader social and sociological influences on the character of the education system.

It is fair to say that there is little to contribute to such an enterprise in the literature on special units which has emerged in a steadily increasing stream during the past decade. Two examples of research which have utilised sociological frameworks are Bird *et al.* (1980) and Tattum (1982), while Galloway *et al.* (1982) have combined sociological with psychological perspectives. These studies have been alive to the schools' institutional characteristics and the pupils' experience of these, while Ford *et al.* (1982) and Tomlinson (1982) have carried out critical examinations of the broader social processes involved in the identification of pupils for various forms of segregated special provision.

A large proportion of the remaining literature is descriptive in character, often in the form of 'success reporting' – accounts of individual projects which seem, to those responsible for them, to have successfully met specific needs in a particular area. Although this material provides useful comparative information about the approaches used, it represents a fragmented and partial view. A number of surveys, which have already been referred to, have provided a more general picture, quantifying the growth as well as describing the range of aims, styles of organisation and methods adopted by units.

Reviews of existing provision have often produced a typology of units based on their location (Wilson and Evans 1980; Dawson 1980; Rabinowitz 1981; Topping 1983). It is less easy to generalise about them on the basis of their philosophies or methods, and the literature reveals a high degree of diversity in this as well as in other features. In one sense the literature portrays the history of many individual searches for appropriate teaching and treatment approaches but it is possible to discern three distinct orientations: therapy, radical social work and education. These are characterised below and references made to examples which broadly reflect them:

1 **Therapy.** This approach sets out to heal the damaged self-concepts of children whose experience of unsatisfactory emotional relationships prevents them from benefitting fully from the opportunities provided by the education system. It is based on psychotherapeutic principles which schools and teachers are able to employ to a limited extent with close guidance and support from outside experts. (Jones 1971, 1973 and 1977; Jones and Davies 1975; Hunkin and Alhadeff 1978; Holman and Libretto 1979.)

2 **Radical social work.** This is an approach which sees the problem as helping the troubled child – who in the context of the education system is an inevitable victim – to cope with his social problems. At the same time it implies a criticism of the system, along with other social institutions, and units in this tradition operate as a form of alternative schooling which seeks to teach the child how to understand and survive his disadvantaged status. (Golby 1978; Grunsell 1978; Taylor *et al.* 1979.)

3 **Education.** In this case the unit strategy is a means of ensuring

that the school can fulfil its obligation to educate even the most problematic of pupils. Special efforts are made to achieve progress in basic elements of the curriculum and to arouse the interest of the pupil in other subjects. The importance of maximising the educational opportunities of all pupils is implied in this approach which has as one of its aims, the intention of ameleorating the situation of teachers and pupils who might otherwise be adversely affected by the disruptive pupil's behaviour. (Chalk 1975; Daniels 1979; Swailes 1979.)

These are tentative and simplified descriptions; they are perhaps best seen as methodological tendencies, operating largely at an ideological level and in practice overlapping to produce a large number of variants.

What is disappointing about the special units literature is the dearth of evaluative studies by means of which the effectiveness of various treatment regimes can be assessed. Topping (1983) has seized upon this weakness and performed the valuable task of scrutinising those English and American studies which provide data amenable to evaluation. His analysis provides a means of comparing the effectiveness of different types of provision for disruptive adolescents classified according to their managerial structures rather than their treatment methods or underlying philosophies. He also compares the efficacy of provision in its many forms with the rate of spontaneous remission which many studies have shown to be a feature of the careers of young people who have been diagnosed as having emotional and behavioural disorders. Topping concludes that special units are among the least adequate of responses to disruption on the basis of their cost-effectiveness.

As in the case of Topping's investigations, there has been elsewhere a widespread preoccupation with administrative and managerial features of unit provision and this probably accounts for another disappointing feature of the literature. With a few notable exceptions (White and Brockington 1978; Grunsell 1978; Grunsell 1980a and 1980b; White 1980; Tattum 1982) the research material projects a rather shadowy image of the young people who populate the units. Often relatively little information is provided about their school careers prior to referral or their perceptions of life within units.

There is frequent recourse in the literature to dichotomous schemes to indicate broad groupings into which the pupils fall.

The most common refers to personality characteristics and behaviour and identifies on the one hand aggressive, extrovert pupils and on the other, the anxious and withdrawn. The range of pupil problems for which units are seen as a suitable response is often reduced to two main forms of deviant behaviour; truancy and disruption and though they are not necessarily mutually exclusive, the indications are that certain pupils have tended to use one or other as a means of expressing their frustration or their estrangement from schools and teachers.

It is for this reason that the term disaffected is preferred to disruptive though it has to be recognised that 'disruptive' is now widely used (as can be seen in contributions in this book) as a more general term. This is not inappropriate provided we recognise that by their behaviour disaffected pupils may not only disrupt the smooth running of classrooms, interfere with the learning of fellow pupils and cause additional stress for teachers, but also disrupt their own educational progress. The consequences of this have been all too often ignored in the existing literature and while the present collection cannot substantially remedy the omission, one of its aims is to draw attention to this aspect of the problem.

The contributing authors include practitioners, researchers and academics, and each presents an individual view informed by his or her particular perspective. Taken together, the collection represents an attempt to analyse the rapid growth of special units from the sociologically informal viewpoint outlined earlier, namely that which sees it as a socially constructed phenomenon of contemporary schooling.

Cathy Bird (Chapter 2) compares the responses to disaffected pupils in a number of schools and illustrates the way in which different strategies reflect different beliefs about the causes of disaffected behaviour, opinions on the relative merits of containment and exclusion, and the availability of resources.

John McDermott, John Leavold and Terry Emerson (Chapters 3, 4 and 5) present detailed case study material to illustrate units in action and to highlight policy issues such as referral and reintegration. From his personal involvement in special units, each writer draws out different questions regarding the purpose of units, their relationship with mainstream schooling, their potential influence upon it and the appropriateness of the policies and methods which have been developed. Chapter 6 (by the editor) is similarly based on empirical data and focuses primarily on the perceptions of a sample of unit pupils, finally considering a number of implications for school policy which can be drawn from their experiences as disruptive or truanting pupils.

The exploration of disruption or disaffection in the remaining three chapters relates the question to broader social, sociological and educational issues. David Coulby (Chapter 7) concentrates on the implications of disruption for the way education is conceived, organised and carried out. Mike Golby and Geoff Whitty (Chapters 8 and 9) both deal with the meaning of the unit phenomenon. The former examines the messages it carries about comprehensive schooling in contemporary society while the latter analyses the ideologies which are apparent in current theory and practice in special units. Together these three chapters provide a radically different interpretation of the growth of units from that found elsewhere in the literature. Accordingly they identify different sets of implications, locating the issue of disaffection firmly in the more fundamental educational debates about the curriculum, assessment and accreditation.

2
The disaffected pupil: a suitable case for treatment?
Cathy Bird

Twenty-five years ago, if a pupil continually misbehaved in school it was likely he would be threatened with the cane. If that failed to curb his bad behaviour, he might have been expelled. The secondary school of the 1980s is supported by special schools, welfare agencies and professional help (see Craft *et al.* 1980; Fitzherbert 1980; Johnson *et al.* 1980; Murgatroyd 1980). The crude measures of past years are no longer the only means of deterring the recalcitrant pupil.

The knowledge that helping agencies are close at hand has an important influence on the ways in which teachers deal with those pupils who find difficulty in adapting to the academic or behavioural standards set by their schools. For example, the presence of local schools for the educationally subnormal, the partially sighted or deaf, which provide an alternative specially formulated education for children with obvious mental or physical difficulties, may prompt teachers to consider referring those pupils who are not getting the most out of their secondary education because of their handicaps. For these children, diagnosis and referral are usually straightforward, although there has been an increasing preference to keep handicapped children within the mainstream of education following the recommendations of the Warnock Report (see Warnock Report 1978; Chazan *et al.* 1980; Swann 1981; Booth and Statham 1982; Brennan 1982; Briggs and Statham 1982).

But for many other pupils, whose 'handicaps' are less clearly identifiable, teachers may have difficulty deciding whether referral is the best kind of help or treatment. A child who perpetually truants or one who is continually disruptive in class may be acting in that way for a variety of reasons, often difficult to diagnose in a clear and concise manner. It has been argued (Booth

1981) that the expansion of special school provision has led teachers in ordinary schools to expect that some of their worst 'problems' can be resolved by removing these pupils on a temporary or permanent basis. 'In such circumstances, special schools (and units) provide educators with the illusion that educational problems are being resolved in such a process and they permit the avoidance of a far more important and challenging issue: how can we meet the needs of all children in our schools' (Booth 1981).

The suggestion that teachers may sweep away some of their most intractable problems by referring their most difficult pupils to special centres or units is in line with one of the many findings of *Disaffected Pupils* (Bird *et al.* 1981) a report of three years' research among pupils and teachers in six schools in two outer London boroughs between 1977 and 1980. It would, however, be wrong to suggest that this was the major way in which the schools resolved the many problems that teachers encountered with some of their most difficult children. It was a useful strategy used only at times of extreme frustration, when all other methods had failed. More often, a caring and thoughtful process accompanied the first administrative steps towards the referral of a pupil from his school to an alternative school or centre, as teachers tried to find explanations for their pupils' disaffection and searched for ways of helping their disruptive, truanting and withdrawn children.

When we looked closely at the referral process in each of the six schools, we found distinct differences between the schools in the number and type of pupils put forward for possible referral. These differences could not be explained by the variety of extra school resources available, the number of vacant places at the centres or units, or any particular characteristics of the pupils attending each school. So why did schools use the available specialist agencies and schools in such different ways?

It was clear that the difference could not be explained simply by the type or availability of specialist help in the two boroughs. Each borough had schools for the educationally subnormal, schools for children with particular physical and mental handicaps, schools for maladjusted children, and psychological assessment centres. There were also home tuition centres, truancy centres and a number of units that dealt with specific behavioural and physical problems on either a long-term or a short-term basis. In both boroughs the educational psychologist served an invaluable function, often acting as a gatekeeper between the schools and the alternative educational centres. Most of the teachers in all six schools recognised the usefulness of educational psychologists, trusting them as professionals who fully understood the educational work of the schools and the individual problems of their pupils.

Yet despite this proliferation of welfare and educational specialists, no two schools used them to the same extent or in the same way.

Three interwoven yet separate reasons for this became evident as we unravelled the referral processes used by each of the six schools. Firstly, no two schools responded to their exceptionally difficult pupils in the same ways, or shared the same ideas about the usual causes of disaffected behaviour. Secondly, no two schools shared the same ideas about the relative merits of referring a child for specialist help, as opposed to containing the child within the school and offering counselling, support or some form of alternative education within the pupil's customary school. And thirdly, each school had a different capability for adapting to or coping with disruptive pupils within the school. In other words, not all schools could stretch their resources to accommodate a child who would not or could not, adapt to the normal rules and standards of the school.

This chapter now turns to a consideration of these three major differences, showing why each school built up unique ways of using the variety of helping and caring agencies that surrounded it.

Institutional theories of disaffection

The first major difference between the schools emerged during the prolonged process of negotiation between the teachers on the exact reasons for the disaffected behaviour of a particular pupil. In some instances, if the behaviour became so severe as to endanger the working of the rest of the class or the school, this discussion process was reduced to a single case conference. In other instances, the process could last a term or more as an increasing number of teachers became enmeshed in sorting out the causes of pupils' disaffected behaviour. The length, depth and content of the discussion in this diagnostic phase differed according to the pupil under consideration and quite fundamentally between schools. Each school had its own particular and often unique interpretation of the principal reasons for disaffected behaviour amongst its pupils. This was not to say that alternative interpretations were never considered or that there was never any dissent amongst the staff on the chief causes of disaffected behaviour. However, it was clear that each school displayed a subtly different institutional view of disaffection, and this affected the chances of any pupil's being referred to an alternative educational centre (Furlong and Bird 1981).

In one school the dominant approach was to see all disaffection as irrational. There was a general belief that any pupil showing signs of anti-school behaviour did not fully appreciate the education that the school offered to him. Counselling and trips to the educational psychologist were seen as soft options; a better way of dealing with such pupils was to bring them swiftly back into line, by whatever means were thought to be most effective. This could mean a series of detentions, a trip to the head teacher's office for some gentle or more physical persuasion, or bringing the pupil's parents into the debate by asking them to back the school in its attempts to get the pupil to conform. Each method was designed to bring the pupil firmly back onto the straight and narrow path of education, from which future deviation would not be tolerated.

In a second school, disaffection was seen as a consequence of the limited educational expectations held by most of its working-class pupils. Teachers saw their role primarily as one of constantly striving to overcome the lack of motivation, the low expectations and the limited aspirations of their pupils. They also directed their attack at the parents of their pupils, whose attitudes often explicitly challenged the need for education and who readily supported their children's attempts to reject or truant from school. Parents were invited into school at every possible opportunity while their children's low aspirations were heightened by a challenging curriculum and dedicated teaching. The school responded to disaffection with a variety of curricula and pastoral methods, combining individual counselling with a more personalised approach to learning, which involved a flexible time-table that allowed certain pupils to work in groups or on their own with an experienced member of staff.

In contrast to these two schools, a third school's interpretation of disaffection was based on the assumption that the majority of disaffection arose from the pupil's personal problems of adjustment to the school. Emotional disturbances were seen primarily as a product of difficulties in their homes. There was a conscious attempt to follow the advice of the educational psychologist who worked closely with the counsellor and senior members of staff. This personalised interpretation of disaffection had consequences for the treatment of disruptive or truanting pupils. The school set up individual time-tables for its most troublesome pupils, gave them as much counselling support as they wanted and tried to adapt the education on offer to fit each individual in whichever way was best suited to his or her emotional make-up. In line with this general philosophy of disaffection, the school had a special unit for a few disruptive pupils. The unit depended on the dedicated perseverance of one teacher who created a family atmosphere within the confines of a small temporary classroom. Here, flexibility of rules and the curriculum were at their most extreme. Each pupil was given an opportunity to work at an individualised work programme within more liberal and adjustable hours of attendance.

These different institutional approaches to the diagnosis of disaffected behaviour meant that the same actions, displayed in different schools, could well be interpreted and treated in radically different ways, depending on the particular explanation adhered to in any one school. It was clear from these alternative approaches that certain school philosophies of disaffection made referral an unnecessary part of the treatment. This was particularly true of those schools which adhered to the 'adolescent rebellion' theory of disaffection, where most bad behaviour could be explained as natural teenage rebellion against adult values and authority. In these schools, the idea of actually referring a pupil to an alternative specialist institution where rules were usually less rigid was seen as giving in to the natural adolescent animosity towards school, work and discipline.

Referral versus containment

The second difference between the six schools in their use of extra-school resources emerged in answer to the question of whether it is better to keep a child within the school system he knows, regardless of his bad behaviour, or to separate him from the school environment, his peer group and the familiar procedures and rules. This argument often ran alongside the previous debate on the reasons for a pupil's disaffected behaviour, merging with it at times of crisis when a decision had to be made quickly on the action to be taken with a particularly difficult child.

As with the alternative theories of disaffection propounded by the different schools, there tended to be an institutionalised view on the containment versus referral debate held by each school, though it was common to hear a variety of alternative ideas put forward in the staffroom. All the schools, however, shared the belief that referral was often inappropriate for disaffected fourth- or fifth-year pupils.

These older pupils usually had clearly defined reasons for their disaffected behaviour, which would have recurred had they been transferred to an alternative educational setting, because it was the actual business of 'being at school' that caused most of them to misbehave. Some felt that the education that they were receiving held little of relevance to their future lives. With jobs already secured, or unemployment an inevitability, some fifth-year pupils saw little reason for conforming to the rules. Other older pupils perceived school as a confining environment, with petty rules and values. They felt that the regulations that governed their behaviour were more suitable for younger pupils and inappropriate for fifteen- and sixteen-year-olds. They considered themselves to be adults and were in fact treated as such outside school. For these pupils, who did not even have a possibility of good examination results as a final prize for five years of conformity, the rules of the school were interpreted merely as frustrating constraints on their freedom.

The reasons for the disruptive behaviour and truanting of these older pupils were generally understood by the majority of their teachers. They recognised that referral for specialist help would be absurd for pupils who had quite clearly grown out of school. The pupils 'wanted out' of the school process and no amount of alternative education could change that. Instead, many attempts were made within the schools to adjust the rules and change the curriculum to suit the needs of this group. Rules of dress were relaxed, teachers tried to adopt different approaches to traditional subjects and the time-table was made as flexible as teacher availability and resources allowed. Some schools worked harder than others at providing a different style of education with the school for their older pupils. Two of the six schools preferred to offer no alternative curriculum, favouring the strategy of persuasion, by suggestion or more physical methods, showing the pupils that conformity to school rules and hard work would give them better prospects and more opportunities for the future than alternative careers of anti-school behaviour or actively refusing to participate in the learning process.

There was less disaffection amongst the younger pupils, but what there was gave rise to much concern amongst the teachers, who could less easily find reasons for their truancy, disruption or withdrawn behaviour. Many of these younger pupils moved in and out of disaffection during their early school careers. In fact, some pupils, defined as disaffected by their teachers at the beginning of our fieldwork, had by the end of our two years in the schools settled completely into their school routines and rarely caused any further trouble. But a few moved progressively from being 'little nuisances' into full-scale problems and it was with these pupils that the question of whether or not to refer usually arose, when all attempts to alleviate their behaviour within the school seemed to have failed.

Schools responded in subtly different ways to the question of whether such pupils should be referred to alternative units or schools or whether they should be contained within the mainstream school and ways found of coping with or adapting the curriculum to the disruptive behaviour. At one extreme was Victoria School, a junior high school taking pupils between the ages of eleven and fourteen. Considerable distance had been established between the school and the special centres and units in the borough. The staff preferred to refer pupils only as a last resort. The headteacher explained:

'I think that there's a danger of almost, if you're not careful, looking for pupils to refer. I would rather start from the stand that we say that we've got a load of kids here, most of whom are normal. There are going to be problems, but basically the school can solve them within its walls ... I'm not prepared to [refer pupils] because I think that referral is an attitude of mind. I'm not convinced that [other alternative centres] can offer anything better than we can.'

This conviction was strongly supported by his staff. They shared a general scepticism about the special education on offer in the borough. Unless recommended to refer a pupil by the educational psychologist, with whom the school had a successful and long-standing relationship, they preferred to contain their problems rather than transfer them elsewhere. As one teacher put it:

'There's a lot of feeling, maybe it's pride, that we'll deal with our own problems rather than pass them on. It's only when we are really desperate that we'll refer ... The only time we really use them is when we want to get them out of our hair. I know that that's the wrong way, but that's how we do it.'

In Victoria School, the question of whether to refer or not was easily resolved by the predominant belief that the school could offer a better alternative education to its difficult children than any other agency or school in the area. The teachers argued that a child may well feel alienated and bewildered by any change of environment. This belief was fuelled by the lack of feedback the staff received about the pupils they had referred and a concern that the psychological or socially based alternative curricula of the special centres and schools offered little of real value for their most disaffected pupils.

In the same borough, Marshbrook School had a completely different view of the usefulness of alternative education for its disaffected pupils. Marshbrook was also a junior high school, feeding the same senior high school as Victoria School. They both served very similar catchment areas. At Marshbrook, the counsellor had an expert knowledge of all the facilities available outside the school and close working links with them. The staff, who greatly valued her judgement, would refer pupils to her, knowing that she would refer them onwards if she felt that the situation demanded it. Her constant personal contact with the specialist centres outside the school reduced any mistrust held by the staff about the workings of the centres and they all felt that referral was the most appropriate treatment for many pupils.

The two schools shared remarkably similar theories on the original reasons for most disaffection – that it was normally the result of their pupils' low expectations and aspirations due to the working-class culture of the area. The differences in their referral procedures were largely a result of their quite separate ideas about whether referral was a suitable means of treatment or whether containment produced a better result. One of the specialist centres, the Heathbury Centre which had recently been set up to deal with the problem pupils of the three schools in the area, including Victoria and Marshbrook, viewed the contrasting approaches of the two schools with concern. The director explained:

'With Victoria we have a sort of crisis intervention, the children who suddenly reached a crisis in the school and have to be moved somewhere else. Then we're brought in. Marshbrook works closely with us, they use us as an extra resource for counselling and giving time to the special needs of individual pupils who have problems.'

The pupils who ended up at the centre displayed quite different degrees and types of disaffected behaviour, depending on the school from which they came, because of the distinctive views held by the two school staffs on the relative merits of referral.

The practical implications of containment

The third difference between the schools in their use of specialist help centred on the overall capability of each school and the school staff to adapt to or cope with disruptive pupils within the context of normal school working. In other words, even when teachers felt fervently that a pupil's behaviour could best be modified or contained within the school, if the resources could not be stretched to cope with the pupil, then there was little alternative but to refer the pupil to another school or unit.

The main practical considerations that influenced their use of the referral process were fourfold: the availability of committed and dedicated teachers who were prepared to teach difficult pupils on their own or within a normal class; the flexibility of the curriculum to allow a small number of children to undertake an altered time-table; the availability of units or special classes specially designed for particular groups of difficult children within the school and lastly, the availability of alternative educational centres outside the school. This last consideration was not a major problem for the schools in the two boroughs where facilities were available for most pupils deemed to be in need of alternative education. The only exception was a truancy centre which was heavily oversubscribed. In cases of truancy, where no alternative could be found for the persistent non-attender the schools had to cope with the problem themselves with the aid of a local educational welfare officer. In some cases, a more attractive strategy was simply to turn a blind eye to truancy, if the pupils could not be persuaded to attend the school regularly.

Making staff available

The availability of staff who were prepared to undertake the separate education of a few severely disaffected pupils within the school was largely dependent on the degree to which the remainder of the staff thought that such use of a teacher's time was a reasonable way of using the school's limited resources. In Victoria School, where there was a clear philosophy that containment was better than referral, all the staff were prepared to increase their own work-load in order to make one senior teacher free at all times to supervise the teaching of any pupil who was misbehaving in lessons. This could mean that an occasional pupil was supervised for the odd lesson or that one particular pupil was supervised for the greater part of his schooling. Similarly, the staff at one of the other schools decided that it was in the best interests of their pupils, and to some extent themselves, to make one teacher free the whole time to supervise a special unit for twelve of the most disruptive pupils in the school. Not only did these arrangements free the rest of the staff at the two schools of their most troublesome pupils; they also allowed the pupils to remain within the school they had grown to know, and at the same time provided them with an education tailored to their particular needs. In both schools, demand occasionally exceeded supply and alternative ways of dealing with the most problematic pupils had to be found. Referral was one answer to this, but both schools resisted this alternative, preferring to keep their most difficult pupils at the school whenever teacher availability and other resources permitted.

Modifying the curriculum

The degree to which the school curriculum could be modified to the requirements of an individual pupil also influenced the chances of a pupil's remaining in the school, rather than being referred elsewhere. In the two junior high schools, where the pupils were between the ages of eleven and fourteen, the curricula were open to considerable variation because neither school was tied to O level or CSE syllabuses. In both schools, where disaffection was seen as stemming from the conflicting values of home and school, the curriculum for the first two years was geared to preparing the pupils for the future rigours of examination work, while also trying to raise the aspirations of the children in the hope of preventing, or at least stemming, the rising tide of school rejection, which was fostered by their home environment and the adolescent culture of their older brothers and sisters. In comparison with these two schools, the curriculum of the senior high school, which took pupils for only their last two years of secondary education, was entirely concerned with O level and CSE syllabuses. There was no room for flexibility to meet the needs of individual or even groups of unco-operative pupils. As one senior teacher put it, 'We prefer the pupils to go through the process of education co-operatively ... but if need be, we drive them through school.'

The dominance of the examination system featured heavily in all the schools that had fourth and fifth years, effectively preventing any great manipulation of the curriculum or time-table to meet the needs of individuals. The only real concession was found in the school that had new facilities and flexible room arrangements. Here pupils could be removed from their exam classes and do the same work under the eye of a senior member of staff. No attempt was made to alter the curriculum to fit the pupil, but the pressure was eased all round by the adoption of this in-school method of individualised learning, while the curriculum remained broadly in line with that on offer to the remainder of the pupils.

Using in-school units

Some of the schools had separate units or special classes specially designed for groups of pupils who were experiencing particular difficulties with their schooling. Mention has already been made of the special unit set up in one school to provide a more personalised form of education for twelve difficult pupils. Other schools had special rooms or classes for ESL teaching and counselling work. Two schools also had West Indian units that were designed to promote West Indian culture. Each school had a remedial department to which some pupils went for special tuition. Although these units and classes were not set up primarily to cope with pupils with behavioural problems, staff often found that a child who was disruptive or who had become a persistent non-attender also had problems with academic work or language, or found difficulty in adapting to the school routines. These extra classes therefore served not only as an additional source of help for particular academic problems but also as behavioural modification units. It was not uncommon to find that particularly difficult pupils had been transferred to them in order to curb their bad behaviour, and also, it must be admitted, to get them out of the way of teachers who could no longer cope with them in their lessons. Similarly, some of the older disruptive children were transferred to the few fourth- and fifth-year

non-examination classes that were available in two of the
schools, not because their level of ability was too low for them to
cope with examination work, but because the classes were to
some extent used as dustbins, taking a residue of pupils that the
examination classes could not contain.

Unofficial ways of coping with disaffection

Running alongside the debate and the practical considerations
that influenced the chances of any one child's being referred to an
alternative school or agency, were a number of unofficial
strategies that had important implications for the treatment of
disaffected pupils within the six schools. These strategies were
sometimes used to cope with disaffection, but did not involve any
real consideration of the reasons for the pupils' behaviour. They
did, however, keep the incidence of pupils who were causing
problems within acceptable limits. Two of these strategies have
already been touched on. Some pupils were referred to units
outside the school, not after careful and thoughtful discussion,
but as a quick method of removing them from the school. Several
truanting pupils were unofficially allowed to get away with very
low levels of attendance as an effective way of keeping class
numbers down and removing those pupils who were usually
gaining little or nothing from their lessons.

In addition to these two strategies, we found a number of other
ways of dealing with disaffection which did not involve any
discussion of the real problem. Some pupils would be thrown out
of classes and told to wait for a senior member of staff in the
corridor. While this procedure worked admirably in schools like
Victoria, where a senior member of staff was on duty at all times,
in other schools it was not uncommon to see many pupils wandering round the corridors or congregating in the toilets during
lesson time, always with the ready-made excuse that they were
looking for a senior member of staff. Another strategy was a form
of barter: teachers would promise that certain pupils need do no
work in lessons as long as they remained quiet.

In each case these unofficial strategies were used by teachers in
order to allow the majority of pupils to work unhindered by the
disruptive few. They also effectively reduced the need to consider
more sophisticated forms of treatment, especially referral which
usually involved considerable time and effort. The strategies also
allowed the younger and more inexperienced teachers to cope
with the hardened trouble-makers without having to resort to

help from a senior teacher and admitting that they were having problems in their classes. This sometimes meant that pupils who should have been withdrawn from lessons remained undiscovered for long periods of time because of a cover-up by those teachers who were using these unofficial strategies to mask the real problems.

A last question

Much hard work and deep, thoughtful discussion usually accompanied the referral of a pupil from his secondary school to an alternative centre or unit. It was a process that involved considerable discussion and action by the staff in all the schools. The different use made of the alternative schools and agencies was determined largely by each school's individual interpretation of disaffection, its views on the relative merits of referral and containment, and its ability to adapt to the individual needs of pupils with behavioural problems. One question remains, however. It is a question which was raised by many teachers in the schools included in our research who, although not arguing against the provision of additional time and resources for disaffected pupils, expressed a concern that the hard-working and conforming pupils were being neglected. If our comprehensive schools are to be promoters of real equality, we must not find ourselves in a situation where some pupils are more equal than others because the scarce resources of educational budgets in the 1980s can only stretch to cover special help for a few children, leaving the rest to fight it out for the remaining teachers and resources.

3
A disruptive pupil unit: referral and reintegration

John McDermott

John at fourteen was considered to be mature for his age, his one ambition was 'to work the fairgrounds'. He had a strong dislike of school and spent as little time there as possible. When he was referred to a unit for disruptive pupils, he had attended school on fifty-four out of 186 possible occasions over the previous six months. His referral followed a suspension from school for what the official record described as 'persistent recalcitrant behaviour'. His parents were in need of help with their son, but school seemed the last place to which they might turn. 'The only time the teachers get in touch is to complain.' John, they felt, had outgrown school.

After the referral, things changed dramatically. His attendance at the unit was good, he seemed to develop self-confidence and he worked hard. Five months later the staff of the unit felt that he was ready for a phased return to school. The school, however, seemed reluctant to provide the work necessary to help this transition and John seemed unhappy at the prospect of returning there. His parents were anxious about his return to 'normal school' because, 'for the first time teachers were saying nice things'.

Attempts were made to get John admitted to two other schools and he was finally admitted to one of them for the last five months of his school career. During this period his attendance and behaviour were good and he followed CSE courses in English, mathematics and art. On leaving school he started work as a lorry-driver's mate.

The research

John was one of six pupils who formed the basis of a study of a unit for disruptive pupils. The unit was one of two set up in the mid-1970s by a local education authority in the north-west of England, to cater for disruptive pupils from its twenty-four secondary schools.

The study, which adopted an interactionist sociological perspective, gathered information through structured interviews. Referred pupils and their parents, unit staff and school staff were asked to talk about the unit and their role in the referral process. The research attempted to describe referral and its consequences for those involved, and to focus attention on what proved to be the most problematic area – that of return to school.

To understand the process which brought certain pupils to the point of referral it is necessary to analyse that process from the point of view of both the teachers (the labellers) and the unit pupils (the labelled). By examining the way in which teachers typify pupils and the way in which negatively labelled pupils react to these typifications, it is possible to gain a sociological insight into the seeming inevitability of the process by which some pupils become designated as 'disruptive'. Formalise this designation by setting up a special unit for disruptive pupils and the process is complete, providing what Hargreaves (1976) called 'the escalator of deviance'.

Any study rests on certain assumptions. Two assumptions in particular should be mentioned here; they are derived from the work of interactionist sociologists whose perspective is essential for any analysis of social processes. The assumptions are broadly in line with labelling theory, as proposed by Becker (1963) and Matza (1964 and 1969).

First, in any situation, especially one of potential conflict like the classroom, the behaviour of all parties must be treated as worthy of investigation. To find the behaviour of certain pupils as in need of explanation, but not that of the teachers who work with them, is illogical. All viewpoints must be taken into account if the label 'disruptive pupil' is to be understood. Secondly, society is made by people. Social categories are created for certain purposes. Thus 'disruptive pupil' is not a mere description of certain pupils but is the outcome of a process by which certain pupil behaviours are labelled.

Hence, in this research, an attempt has been made to look at the three groups involved: school teachers, unit staff and referred pupils. It views each as actively defining their situation: the pupils concerned with certain things and acting to meet those concerns, the unit staff as actively trying to implement their ideas of 'treatment', and the school staff as actively making pupil referrals on the basis of a pathological type (i.e. the 'disruptive pupil') and ready to receive the returned pupil, after 'treatment' in the unit.

The research model adopted is based on that exemplified in Goffman's classic study, 'The moral career of the mental patient' (1961). This presented a clear sense of process and his terminology – 'pre-patient', 'in-patient' and 'ex-patient' – was appropriate to phases in the careers of unit pupils. In choosing the research sample it was decided that to select from the pre-patient phase would pre-empt referral in its attempt to isolate potentially 'disruptive pupils'. The in-patient phase was clearly the least problematic, but the sample chosen consisted of the last six pupils to be returned from the unit to normal schooling. This ex-patient phase was also emerging as the most problematic area for all concerned. As Erikson (1964) observed, the status transformation caused by labelling someone in a public ceremony is difficult to reverse if that society does not provide a terminal ceremony to signify a shift out of the deviant role. This was clearly in evidence for pupils returning from a period in the unit.

In this chapter it is intended to show, by an analysis of the research material, that the referral process is arbitrary, based as it is on teachers' interpretations of the term 'a disruptive pupil'; that respondents have their own perspectives on events and a lack of appreciation of the perspectives of the others involved; and that the resulting poor communication and problems of liaison were most pronounced at the point when the pupils were being prepared for a return to school.

The nature of the unit

The unit which forms the basis of this study is one of two set up by the LEA in the mid-1970s to cater for an increasing number of pupils whose behaviour was considered too disruptive for normal school. The aim was to make some form of educational provision available for these pupils, in the hope that, after a suitable period of time, they could be returned to their school of origin. Each unit was set up in buildings independent of its feeder schools with up to four members of staff.

Admission to the unit was initially intended to be restricted to children not attending school and who had not attended school for some time. Pupils were to be referred by schools, by any of the agencies working in the field, the education department or they could be self-referred. Children were to be admitted in consultation with the head of the school, members of the local inspectorate and officers of the education committee – the placement of each pupil being open to review at least once each term. It is significant that one of the aims of the units was to prepare pupils 'for a return to normal schools'. One of the criteria of acceptance by the units was that the child remain on the register of the referring school.

In the unit the teaching method was based on classroom techniques. In addition a points system operated, so that the behaviour of each pupil was closely monitored. At the time of the study there were three qualified teachers working in the unit with eighteen pupils. The tutor-in-charge was concerned to develop a relationship of trust between the adults and the pupils in the unit. The atmosphere was consequently less formal than that of a normal school but nevertheless there was a definite structure and pupils were expected to adhere to this at all times.

The unit operated along what was described by the staff as 'behaviour modification lines', using the peer group as well as the staff as monitors of pupil progress. Marks were given for each session in the day and these were displayed in graph form. A group meeting every Friday allowed the pupils to comment on one another's progress. At the end of the meeting pupils would select two specific areas of their own behaviour upon which they would concentrate for the next week. These then became the basis of group monitoring throughout the following five days.

The labelling process

As outlined earlier, labelling theory would suggest that deviance is seen as a question of social definition and that it is a relative phenomenon.

> If a deviant act is an act that breaks some rule, since rules vary between different cultures, subcultures and groups, acts which are deviant (i.e. which break rules) in one culture, sub-culture or group may not be deviant in another culture, sub-culture or group. (Hargreaves 1975)

This focus on the relative nature of deviant labels and of labelling draws attention to the problematic nature of the term 'disruptive pupil' and to the relative power differential between the labelled (the pupils) and the labellers (the teachers). It also raises questions about the relative capacity of pupils and teachers to impose their definitions on the situation in general and on specific acts in particular. When a rule is broken in the classroom the teacher can be seen as victim, prosecutor, judge and executioner. Furthermore, the whole process from the detection of rule breaking to the teacher's judgement and treatment can be condensed into an event of two or three seconds duration. Hargreaves (1975) considers the operation of this process: 'In classrooms we are often concerned with what we might term 'routine deviance' – the rapid 'processing' by the teacher of common and minor breaches of the rules.' It is through this process that the teacher moves from deviant acts (e.g. talking, cheating or bullying) to deviant persons (e.g. chatterbox, cheat or bully). The process therefore induces teachers to recognise pupils as certain kinds of persons. Hargreaves describes this by means of the concept of 'typification' (taken from the work of Schutz 1944 and 1973) which explains how one person perceives, categorises or types another.

Becker (1952) argued that teachers have an image of the ideal client against which actual clients are evaluated as 'good' or 'bad'. Similarly Hargreaves sees a process of typification which culminates in a stage of stabilisation which is then resistant to change. The negatively or positively labelled pupil is 'acting out of character' if he does not conform to the perceived view of him. At this point the pupil is said to be stigmatised and is seen by his teacher as a 'problem pupil'. Thus the teacher transforms his conception of the pupil; he was once 'normal' but now he is 'deviant'. Once the pupil is defined as deviant he will tend to be treated as untrustworthy and as a target of suspicion. His accounts of himself will be carefully checked. He is not allowed to be above suspicion like a 'normal' pupil. In addition he may be isolated or excluded for fear that he will affect his peers – hence special units.

Thus the deviant pupil is labelled and isolated. This process is furthered by the pupil's own reaction to his situation. The work of Lemert (1951) and Matza (1964) suggests that initially the commission of deviant acts has only marginal implications for the person committing them, especially if the acts are undetected or considered 'out of character'. However, when there is a social reaction to the deviance which creates a problem for the person who committed the act, which he chooses to resolve by the commission of further deviant acts, the motive for the deviance has changed. The social reaction which was intended to control the situation has exacerbated it. It is a short step, in school terms, to the search by the deviant pupil for social support for his deviance.

The problematic nature of the word 'disruptive' was apparent throughout the research. It was obvious that teachers did not have a clearly defined idea of what constituted a 'disruptive pupil'. Replies to the question 'What is meant by teachers when they talk about "disruptive" pupils?' are illustrated by the following:

'Anyone who prevents a normal class operating.'

'Someone who will not allow a lesson to continue properly.'

'Someone who is not psychologically disturbed but just badly behaved.'

'Abnormal behaviour of any kind.'

Clearly teachers interpret pupil behaviour in a variety of ways and even if a common description of a 'disruptive pupil' could be agreed on, it would still be open to endless interpretations in terms of quality and degree.

This is further complicated by the fact that teachers often describe pupil behaviour as deviant even though they may not always take action because the act of deviance is very minor. The cumulative result of these minor acts is a vague impression that a particular pupil is deviant. This tends to lead to generalised labels such as 'difficult', 'a problem', 'unco-operative'.

The teachers, when asked about the pupil before referral to the unit, made similar generalised responses:

'Basically non-co-operative.'

'A constant disrupter.'

'He was quietly self-willed.'

'He was a thorough-going nuisance.'

'She just enjoyed disrupting the school.'

None of these statements gives any clear indication of the acts that the pupil commits. When pressed, the teachers used more specific labels to talk about the pupils in detail, but it was a general label such as 'difficult' which seemed to summarise the teachers' conception of the 'disruptive' pupil. It is this generalised labelling which passes around in staffroom discussion and forms the basis of the typing of a particular pupil as potential 'trouble'.

The literature shows that, in the main, pupils tend to see their deviance as 'situational', while teachers often see it as 'pathological'. In this study there is a further complication. In the unit, the staff do, on occasions, refer to a pupil in terms of 'pathologies', whilst also seeing the pupil's difficulties in school as 'situational'. The resulting ambivalence is illustrated in the way unit staff defined one pupil's problem *vis-à-vis* his school: 'He was essentially a school refusal problem.' 'Eric's problem was truancy.'

These two remarks indicate a lack of certainty as to who has the problem. Whilst the pupils are clear that it is they who find school a problem, the unit staff seem to alternate between describing pupils as having a problem with school – 'Eric's problem was truancy' – and the school authorities as having a problem with the pupil – 'He was essentially a school refusal problem'. This ambivalence is obviously a factor in any explanation of the lack of positive contacts with the main school. The staff of the unit are not seen by the schools as necessarily supportive.

Support, in the school's terms, is to agree with its diagnosis of the pupil and react to it as the school would do. The staff of the unit feel the need to sympathise with the referred pupil, as they have to build a working relationship with him or her. Furthermore, the pupils and the staff of the unit agree that there is a problem with 'school' in general, and with a return to school in particular. The teacher in charge of the unit made this comment:

'Our biggest problem is encouraging contact with schools. We have lots of social workers and educational welfare officers popping in, but very few teachers. Few schools ever bother even to ring up.'

A further aspect of labelling revealed in the study is highlighted by the comments of one referred pupil, Tony, when he said of his school: 'The teachers didn't like me because of our kid. She was trouble in school and so they thought I was.' This raises the question of the 'sibling phenomenon' in imputations of deviance in school (Seaver 1973).[1] Three of those interviewed felt that their 'unfair' treatment was based on the assumption that they would display similar traits to those shown by an older sibling. In each case the pupils felt that the staff were 'picking' on them, although they were all careful to point out that their problems were not with all the teachers but with the ones to whom they found it difficult to relate.

'I couldn't get on with some of 'em.' (John)

'They all picked on me for nothing.' (Tony)

'As soon as I walked in he was on to me.' (Sue)

'Some of them did nothing but shout at you.' (Eric)

'Some of them just looked down on you.' (Phil)

'I got on with some of them and either ignored the others or answered them back.' (Steve)

Most schools contain a variety of teachers with very different social, political and educational philosophies. We often give them loose labels such as 'traditionalists' and 'progressives'. Accordingly, their concepts of a deviant pupil and of classroom behaviour differ. Those who wish to preserve the status differential will inevitably define some pupil conduct as cheeky, whereas the teacher who is trying to play down this status differential will describe the same behaviour as 'natural', 'open' or even 'friendly'.

Jordan's (1974) study of teacher types showed sharp contrasts. The first type of teacher saw deviant pupils as anti-authority, anti-work and anti-social. He was inconsistent in his punishments, made derogatory remarks about such pupils and refused to believe that any signs of improvement were authentic. The second type believed that these pupils really wanted to work and encouraged them. He was consistent and avoided confrontation, praising any sign of improved performance.

In the present study, the teacher interviews were directed towards other issues and such sharp differences were not detected. However, the distinction made by Jordan can be related to the present analysis. There were clear indications that in some schools used in the study, the prevailing ethos was more towards the first type – the 'deviance-provocative' stance. The comments of one year tutor serve to illustrate this point:

'The boy is in an impossible situation [part-time at school and part-time in the unit]. He lacks the character to make the adjustment between the disorganised atmosphere of the unit and the controlled environment of school. These kids in particular should be in a controlled situation. They have got to fit into society and this [the unit] will not help.'

It seemed that the school was not prepared to meet the unit and the pupil other than on its own terms and according to its own rules. As a result the part-time arrangement failed. The boy was finally excluded from school for failing to attend an accumulation of three detentions, given because he had failed to comply with the school rules regarding uniform.

The referral procedure

In setting up the unit, the unit staff had been careful to follow the procedure for referral as originally laid down by the education committee. However, in reality it was often difficult for staff in schools to understand why certain pupils were referred. The arbitrary nature of the process was often indicated in the interviews with teachers:

'We have far worse problems still at school.'

'By no means was he our worst problem.'

'I was surprised when I heard that he had been referred.'

It was never very clear just how certain pupils were processed and not others. In this context it is worth noting that, in setting up the unit, the authority was intending to cater for twenty-five pupils in total. The working party of headteachers and education committee officers who recommended the setting up of such units had estimated a need in terms of one hundred and fifty pupils. There may be more than a little truth in the comment of one deputy headmaster when he said, 'No matter how many units the authority creates, the schools will fill them.'

At the time of the study, the unit was temporarily undersubscribed despite the fact that each school visited indicated that it had potential referrals. This was due to a combination of factors connected with the referral procedure, in particular a deliberate policy on the part of the education committee to allow the unit to develop in a planned way, together with a lack of understanding amongst schools about how referral was to be brought about.

Often, it seems, the fact that a certain pupil reaches the point of being referred to a unit has less to do with the severity of his misdemeanour than with the stage in the term or school year and the state of what might be described as 'staff morale'. In the sample, four out of six initial referrals were made in the summer term (cf. Lawrence et al. 1978).[2]

The events leading up to the referral of each member of the sample illustrated a whole 'career' of developing deviance, the culmination of which was the deviant act committed immediately prior to the pupil's suspension. Interestingly, it was this final act which the pupil mentioned when asked the question 'What led to your being suspended from school?'

'I had a fight with another girl in the toilets.' (Sue)

'I didn't go to school.' (Eric)

'I threatened a teacher.' (John)

'I went into the swimming pool area through the boiler-house.' (Steve)

'I was sent to the deputy head 'cause I hadn't got a pen and he slung me out.' (Tony)

'I squared up to one of the teachers.' (Phil)

The teachers, when asked the same question, related a whole sequence of problems. Sue's headmaster, describing events leading up to her referral, said:

'Prior to being referred, Sue had a long history of disrupting lessons, wandering around class, being rude and abusive and getting into fights with other girls. Her problems seemed to be connected to her over-identification with a twin sister, coupled with the ineffectiveness of parental control.'

Sue agreed that she had been a problem in school right through from the middle primary years. She had been suspended on several earlier occasions. The headmaster admitted that in referring Sue, the school had failed, but he felt that he had to support his staff and give them a break and believes that it was unfair that Sue should continue to disturb the school's normal functioning.

John was described by his year tutor as 'basically non-co-operative. He was frequently late, never completed homework and refused to wear the school uniform.' John felt that things were not as difficult in the first and second years: it was in the third year that things started to go wrong. He felt that certain teachers were picking on him and he began to dislike school. By the time he reached the fourth year he was regularly in trouble and felt that he was no longer given a chance. What he resented most was the fact that staff used the reputation of an older sibling as evidence that he was a 'bad lot'. He was referred to the unit after what the deputy headmaster described as 'a rather unsavoury incident in which he threatened a young member of staff'.

Tony was at the same school as John and in the same year group. He too felt that things went reasonably well in the first and second years. In the third year things 'got worse with the staff' and school became 'a bore'. When the staff shouted at him, he felt picked on and shouted back. An older sibling with a bad school reputation was again seen as being used against him: 'When they realised I was her brother, they never let me forget it.' According to the deputy headmaster: 'He was a nuisance, was unpleasant and anti-authority.' It would seem that a difference of opinion between the boy's mother and one of the school staff, which almost came to blows, was not unconnected with the boy's referral. The deputy headmaster went on to explain that 'Tony had refused to wear his uniform and conform to normal school discipline and was a bad example to the others'.

In the case of Steve, the senior master claimed that

'Steve was a constant problem in school, disrupting some lessons by making silly noises and setting up difficult situations for the staff. [Steve claimed that he only did this to those he did not like.] He was also a problem out of lessons, being responsible for vandalism around the school, and was frequently involved in fights.'

The final suspension of Steve from his school was a direct result of pressure by one of the teachers' unions in the school. One of the incidents had led to Steve's 'squaring up' to a member of staff, at a time when that particular union was 'making a stand' against acts of violence against teachers. Hence the headmaster felt he had no alternative but to exclude the boy and insist on his referral or transfer to another school.

Phil had a history of lateness, missing lessons and being rude and abusive when checked. He accepted that he was a problem for his school, although things had been better in first and second years. He felt that his problems were only with a few staff with whom he did not get on very well. However, the unit staff explained that Phil had been referred to the Child Guidance Clinic and that their reports indicated attacks on other pupils and general aggressive behaviour as the reason for referral. The deputy headmistress agreed: 'The final suspension did result from rude behaviour following an incident, involving Phil and another boy, over equipment in a practical lesson.'

Once again the time of year seems to have been an important factor. The deputy headmistress continued:

'It was about this time in the term [June] and people were tired. It was at a time when there was some discussion of teacher assaults and feelings were running high. We felt that to suspend Phil would have the effect of calming the situation. Also his parents saw it as a way of smoothing things over.'

Eric was referred by the Child Guidance Clinic for non-attendance at school. He was in no way disruptive and the school staff were surprised that he should have been referred to a unit for disruptive pupils. Talking with Eric revealed that he did not like school as he found it difficult to get on with the other pupils and the staff. He therefore spent long periods of time truanting. The Child Guidance Clinic, which only operated in the mornings, felt that he needed full-time accommodation in a small group and in a sympathetic atmosphere – hence their decision to refer him. His year tutor said, 'I was frankly shocked that he had been transferred. His problem was non-attendance, not bad behaviour.'

It would seem, therefore, that there existed no coherent social view behind the decision of school staff members and child guidance counsellors in making referrals to the unit. The main discernible reason appears to have been the variety of interpretations of the word 'disruptive', coupled with the timing of these events in terms of the school year.

Adjustment to the unit

When pupils were accepted into the unit there was a period of adjustment followed by a determination to make a successful return to 'normal' school. As the teacher in charge of the unit explained:

'We do not always see the problem expressed by the school; once they settle the pupils see it [the unit] as one big family. They enjoy being here but do want to get back. That [their previous school] is 'normal', here they are "special".'

For the pupils this early period of adjustment to their new environment was not easy. The early days were usually characterised by the pupil's being quiet and withdrawn. The unit staff were rarely able to identify the problem described by the school staff. Only one of the six pupils, Tony, displayed the temper tantrums and anti-social behaviour reported by his school.

The settling in process was conducted against a background of concerns in the pupil's home, about having been 'expelled from normal school' or 'being too bad for ordinary school', and the worry of 'What will the neighbours think?'. This, together with the taunts of friends about going to a 'special' school, made for quite considerable problems of adjustment.

Steve's friends referred to the unit as 'the mong school', whilst Phil and Sue both faced comments about 'a school for nutters'. The pupils were keen to point out that they did not think that they were any worse than a number of others in their peer group:

'Some of me mates started saying it's a school for mad people and I said it was for difficult kids ... but a lot of others were bad at school and they only got rid of me.' (John)

'When I first went to [the unit] I kept thinking that there's worse than me at school and they haven't been chucked out.' (Steve)

The sharp contrast between the unit and the secondary schools, in terms of size, personnel, buildings, equipment and organisation was something which the unit staff had taken into account in the development of its identity and in the pursuance of its aims. However, for both pupils and school staffs, these differences could be disconcerting. For the pupils the unit had the appearance of a soft option – something they tended to play up with their peers to counter the taunts about 'special' schools, as Phil explained: 'I thought, this is OK, drinking tea and swearing, suits me!' Steve saw it as 'pretty cool. They were all lounging around and that.'

However, this first impression did not help the settling-in process. Without exception, those interviewed expressed difficulties and apprehensions about moving into this new situation. There was the almost inevitable 'challenge' by one of the existing group. Sue thought that she must have created the wrong impression in the first few days, as she explained: 'I suffered a lot of aggro and stayed away in the second week.' The staff were sensitive to Sue's difficulties and were able to discuss with her the social problems relating to settling into a new group. It took them two weeks to persuade Sue to make a second attempt and in the meantime they were able to use the weekly meetings at the unit to help prepare the rest of the group for Sue's return.[3]

Once settled in the unit, the pupils enjoyed the routine. It was clear in all the interviews that not only were they able to point to differences between school and unit, but they were much more sensitive to and aware of what was happening at the unit. The organisation and routines of school were not as clear and understandable to them.

John felt that, in the unit, he was always aware of the points system: 'Even though you pretended not to be worried, you still tried.' In his school he felt unsure of where he stood, except that he had a reputation which he felt always held, even with a new teacher: 'If you did something wrong they wouldn't let you forget it. At the unit, after something had been sorted out, it was forgotten.' John, like the others, commented on how the unit dealt with a pupil who arrived late and how he found the weekly meetings:

> 'I liked the daftness of it. If you were late they sent you home but they [the pupils] did not like it. I know it sounds crazy but it worked. The Friday talks were brilliant. They showed who was who. Originally you felt frightened but then everyone pitched in. If they said something was wrong you would think about it and if they said good things you were chuffed. It sort of built up trust.'

Phil saw these sessions as helping to 'find out what others thought of me. It was not always nice but it was good to learn it.' Eric thought a good deal before declaring, 'They [the Friday sessions] sort of gave me courage.'

Despite feelings of hostility towards the teachers in their former schools, their feelings for the staff at the unit were very different. They saw them as being friendly, fair and concerned.

> 'You can have a joke with them.' (John)

> 'They're always straight with you.' (Steve)

> 'They're interested in you as a person. They are not so formal in the unit, you can talk to them. In school they [the teachers] are very impersonal.' (Sue)

The staff at the unit felt that the atmosphere of 'one big family' that they created was crucial to working with pupils who had 'problems'. Certainly, this philosophy worked in that the pupils were happy and responsive. However, in terms of their primary aim of returning pupils to their school of origin, it was this very philosophy which seemed to place a barrier between the school and the unit. So it was no surprise to find the return to school emerging as the most problematic stage of the whole process.

The school's attitude to the unit

The antipathy felt by the school teachers to the unit's philosophy meant that there was little meaningful dialogue between schools and the unit. In the interviews with teachers in the schools, those who had visited the unit were disconcerted by what they saw. They were sending pupils who were, in their estimation, undisciplined, anti-authority and generally out of control. They hoped that through referral, the pupils would become disciplined and more conformist before being returned to school. In the unit, it seemed that their worst fears were being realised. These pupils, instead of being prevented from indulging in the worst excesses of adolescent behaviour, were allowed to do all those things that the school had been struggling to prevent them from doing. John's year tutor compared the school and unit as

> 'two different cultures on different wavelengths ... When I visited the unit I was shocked. I did not agree with either the principles or the practices ... It was not what I would call a working situation, it was a disorganised establishment. These kids, in particular, should be in a controlled situation. They need very firm supervision.'

Sue's headmaster also visited the unit and was

> '... frankly horrified ... I have been a headmaster for twenty years and in all that time I have never been spoken to as I was by one of those boys when I first walked into the unit ... Their attitude to staff was so casual ... I do not wish to go again.'

This negative reaction from school staff has, of course, to be balanced against what the unit staff see as the obvious gains of such an approach. A major benefit lies in the very positive relationships between pupils and staff who have a clear commitment to seeing life from the pupil's point of view. However, for the staff of the unit, this is a dilemma; on the one hand, the success of their methods adds force to the belief that many of the pupil's problems in school are 'situational'. On the other, if they are to appear as successful, they must enable their pupils to return to an unchanged situation in school where the pupil's deviance is seen as 'pathological'.

Reintegration

Interviews with staff in the referring schools revealed apprehension about having pupils back. While the teachers appreciated the need for a phased return, they each pointed out that their time-table made it difficult for any pupil to attend on only certain days of the week. Furthermore, it was not always easy for them to provide appropriate school work for pupils to do in the unit. The arrangements made by schools for the return of a pupil varied. Some made a place available in the appropriate year group and placed the pupil 'as if he had never been referred'. Others took 'some care to provide appropriate lessons to allow him to settle in'.

Sue attempted a return to her school after three months in the unit. Arrangements were made for her to go into school two days each week. According to the headmaster it failed because 'Some of the staff were trigger-happy where Sue was concerned'. Sue felt, in retrospect, that she could not cope with the problems it presented: 'I had older friends who, because of the rules, I could not meet at lunchtime.' A teacher she did not like also seemed to play a significant part in the problems which built up. After three weeks the plan had to be abandoned and Sue returned full-time to the unit. After a further ten months, and with some apprehension, the part-time arrangement was reintroduced and was still in operation and being seen as reasonably successful at the end of the research period.

Tony started a part-time return to his school after fourteen months in the unit and was attending full-time at school after a further five months. However, by this time he was in his fifth year. He felt out of his depth in the classes he attended and had become a fairly persistent truant.

Phil returned part-time to school after twelve months in the unit. By this time he was starting his last year at school. A reluctance on the part of his school to accept him other than on a part-time basis meant that a return as a full-time pupil was not achieved before he finally left school.

Steve started a part-time return to school after only two months at the unit. Looking back, the staff of the unit felt that this was too soon, but it had been justified on the grounds of 'remarkably good behaviour'. This Steve put down to sheer determination: 'I knew I had to be good to get back to school, so that's what I meant to do.' It all failed when Steve got into further trouble at school. In Steve's terms, he was set up by other pupils in his peer group. According to the unit staff, some of the staff of the school never gave him a chance: 'It was a question of a leopard not being able to change its spots.' Following his return to the unit full-time, his work and attitude changed dramatically and his attendance was poor. This change in attitude and the refusal of the school to try again meant that he finally reached the statutory school leaving age whilst still full-time in the unit.

Eric started a part-time return to school after twelve months and this became full-time after a further three months. Eric put this down to meeting new teachers in the upper part of his comprehensive school.

Each pupil was well aware of the difficulties of returning as the following comments show:

'I would worry the day before I went to school that it would go OK. (Sue. When part-time in school.)

'I knew going back wouldn't be easy but they didn't give me a chance.' (John)

'Some of the staff and even some of the kids didn't give me a chance.' (Steve)

'They [the school teachers] were just the same, ready to pick on me for nothing.' (Tony)

'I felt some [of the teachers at school] tried but most didn't want to give me a chance to show I'd changed.' (Phil)

'It was OK with the teachers I didn't know.' (Eric)

This attitude of genuine concern about their situation was clear throughout the interviews and points up a crucial area of difference between the schools and the unit in terms of how each perceived the attitude of the pupils to referral. The teachers in the schools tended to feel that the pupils enjoyed being in the unit and saw referral as a kind of triumph over the system. Tony's year tutor claimed, 'At the unit the kids obviously see that they have won. The school imposed discipline, they flouted it and got away with it.' The teacher in charge of the unit summed up this attitude:

'I think they [the teachers] really feel that these kids would rather be here. In truth they want to get back to a 'normal' school. If going back to school fails, then this can be catastrophic for the individual. He sees himself as a failure, not as having triumphed over the system. It requires a lot of PR work with the schools.'

Certainly the comments of the pupils bear this out:

'You're sort of branded, aren't you, when you're here [at the unit].' (Tony)

'I want to leave from a normal school. You can't write where it says "school last attended" – a school for disruptive kids – can you?' (Sue)

'It was important to me to go back and leave from a normal school.' (Phil)

'If you didn't get back [to school] everybody would think you was a real bad lot.' (John)

'I don't stand a chance [of a job] if I leave from here [the unit].' (Steve)

Conclusion

Special units for disruptive pupils are a recent phenomenon in the field of secondary education. It will be some considerable time before their contribution can be accurately assessed. Her Majesty's Inspectorate of Schools, in their report on 'Behavioural Units' (DES 1978b), started this work by trying to assess the nature of and procedures employed by those units already in existence.

The findings of the research reported above have borne out the conclusions of the HMI report. This particular off-site unit is in no way atypical; the pupils, school teachers and staff from the unit have indicated in their interviews that they face the same problems as those outlined in the report.

The label 'disruptive pupil' seems to imply certain basic assumptions:

1 That there are children who are disruptive *per se*, and once recognised as the devils they are, they simply need to be excluded from the classroom.

2 That the 'disruptive pupil' can be clearly recognised as a special case and therefore obviously different from the 'normal learner' in any classroom.
3 That disruption is always a bad thing and what is being disrupted is always good.
4 That a major school problem will be solved if the classroom teacher identifies the disruptive child and gets him excluded.

Each of these assumptions takes for granted the neutrality of the teacher and the school. This research has questioned these assumptions and shown the part played by the teacher and the school. It has attempted to show the arbitrary nature of the term 'disruptive pupil' and of the process by which certain pupils become so designated.

There is little doubt about the success of the unit in creating a caring atmosphere and in improving the attitude and behaviour of the individuals who have been referred. Whether, however, it has achieved its stated aims or, indeed, can ever achieve them in its present form, is open to question. The fundamental problem relates to the arbitrariness and relative nature of the criteria by which pupils come to be referred. The unit has to deal with pupils who are referred on the basis of the school's estimation of what is unacceptable behaviour. The criteria for this estimation are out of the hands of those in charge of the unit, and similarly the criteria by which the pupil will be judged on his return to school cannot be easily influenced by the staff at the unit. Hence the unit is operating in a vacuum. The pupil is referred on the basis of his failure to meet the behavioural standards set by his school. He is, however, judged ready for a return to school on the basis of his success in meeting behavioural standards acceptable in the unit – standards which are, by the nature of the institution, different from those demanded in school.

During the course of conducting the interviews the writer visited only five of the twenty-four potential feeder comprehensives. Even within this small sample, the difference in teacher attitudes, behavioural expectations and prevailing ethos was quite significant. In these circumstances the problems inherent in the unit model are increased.

To complicate the situation further, the teachers in the schools seemed unclear about the procedure for referring pupils to the unit. They also found it difficult to place the unit in relation to the other support agencies, such as the Child Guidance Service.

Above all, they seemed ignorant of the unit's role in the education service and of the methods it had adopted.

Despite the fact that many teachers seemed unaware of the referral procedure it was a fairly complex and lengthy process. A special committee was convened; reports were requested from the school and any social agency involved with the pupil; the pupil and his or her parents visited the unit and the staff at the unit visited the home. For the pupil to change from 'normal' school to the 'special' unit was very clearly marked. In Garfinkel's (1956) terms a 'degradation ceremony' was undertaken. The return to normality was, by contrast, marked by little fuss and ritual, perhaps a further reason for the difficulties encountered in returning pupils to normal schooling. As Scott and Douglas (1972) point out:

> In this regard it is interesting to note that most normal agencies of social control in our society appear to be better equipped for detecting, apprehending and confining the deviant than they are at bringing him back from the institution to the centre of the community.

In a similar vein, Mechanic (1968) has suggested that most social control agencies employ a far larger number of people to process clients into them, than they do to process clients back out.

The over-riding feature of the process of referral examined above is that of poor communication between the organisations and individuals involved. Despite the good work being done with individual pupils, the unit has failed to explicate its purpose and methods.

The schools have failed to examine the process of deviance which brings the disruptive pupil to the point of referral. It may be that the answer to the problem of disruptive behaviour lies not in off-site units but in further research in classrooms, with regard to curriculum and management strategies. The application of the labelling perspective to classroom deviance leads us to ask which teacher reactions are most likely to reduce subsequent deviance rather than promote or confirm it.

Since labelling theory implies an analysis of how people come to be labelled deviant, it also offers some potential methods for reducing deviance. One possibility, as Hargreaves (1975) suggests, would be to label the act rather than the person, thus giving the person the chance to normalise his conduct:

If teachers could systematically, and from an early stage, focus their deviant definitions on acts rather than persons, then many of those processes which facilitate deviant pupil careers, especially the teacher's typing of a pupil as deviant, could be powerfully inhibited.

Until this happens, the problems outlined will continue to place constraints on the development of the unit and the success with which it can carry out its stated aims.

In the process of withdrawing pupils from school to a special unit, a number of problems have been identified:

1 A disparity between the official philosophy of the unit and what in fact happens.
2 The need to reconcile the approach adopted in the unit with the expectations of staff in the feeder schools.
3 The lack of consensus on what constitutes acceptable behaviour in general and 'disruptive' behaviour in particular.
4 The need to explicate the purposes and procedures of the unit and to begin to acknowledge the enormity of its task.
5 The need to reconcile the pupils' 'situational' understanding of behaviour problems with the 'pathological' approach of the teachers.

The first of these problems hinges on whether the unit is seen as 'therapeutic' or 'correctional'. The teacher-in-charge of the unit expressed the official philosophy in terms of help with problems: 'The children come to us with various behavioural, emotional and social problems ... Our job is to help them to get better adjusted to themselves and others.' However, the schools referred pupils for correctional reasons. The pupils were unable to behave properly and were expected on their return to be changed and to have realised the folly of their ways. Similarly, the pupils were clearly of the opinion that they were sent to the unit for not behaving themselves. The unit, despite what it sees as its main purpose, has set itself behavioural criteria for a return to school. The pupils must score points which are based on their ability to be good, hardworking, sociable and co-operative.

The lack of consensus between the teachers in the different schools as to what constitutes deviant behaviour is obviously of major significance. What may appear outrageous under one regime may be mildly amusing under another. As research shows (e.g. Werthman 1963; Jordan 1974), the type of teacher and their reactions to deviant acts can be crucial. Some reactions provoke further deviance. There is much research evidence on the area of classroom interaction, but teachers in general seem unwilling or unable to develop the skills which have been shown to be essential to their craft. This may, as Hargreaves (1972) has suggested, be due to the lack of a theoretically based professional language through which they might begin to explicate, in an objective way, elements of classroom interaction. The development of such a language would help in the identification of elements of successful practice. This would also help the unit in its efforts to encourage a more meaningful dialogue with the schools. As with much of teachers' 'recipe knowledge' the purposes and procedures of the unit are assumed rather than explicated and understood.

For the staff of the unit, the major problem is how to convince the school teachers that their 'pathological' view of the deviant is an inappropriate model for an understanding of the referred pupil. The school teachers have the vast majority of 'normal' pupil reactions as proof that the acts of the 'disruptive' pupil are characteristic of the individual rather than a reaction to a specific situation. There is a need to recognise and understand the interactive nature of problems in school and

> to acknowledge their relativity in so far as who and what is unacceptable. In particular, there is a need for constructive action based on the specific acts of children rather than on the general type of pupil they are perceived to be. (Seaver 1973)

This implies greater objectivity, more experimentation and regular evaluation when faced with continuing problems. Some established conceptual frameworks currently being used by teachers are clearly in need of modification.

These tentative research findings point to a number of possible policy changes for those involved with the unit. There is a need for a carefully planned programme to explain the purpose of the unit and the procedures for admission. The unit staff might consider making moves towards more meaningful dialogue with schools, possibly by a programme of staff exchanges and by more formalised in-service training, at which the question of a 'professional' language might be raised. Finally, and perhaps most important, there might be a reconsideration of the aim of returning pupils to their school of origin. It is clear that this is the major stumbling block of the whole referral process. Perhaps pupils should be placed in a different school. This would present the possibility of a fresh start and would, for all concerned, allow for a 'ceremonial' of acceptance of the 'disruptive' pupil back into a 'normal' school situation. This would have to be very carefully organised and would raise the whole question of how much knowledge of the pupil the receiving school should have access to. At this stage such a move might break the circular process of the deviant career of the 'disruptive' pupil.

However, having made these observations, the writer is aware that they imply changes in our schools of a kind which are most unlikely. Why should high-status organisations like schools make changes to accommodate low-status individuals like the 'disruptive' pupil? In the meantime there is a need for the caring atmosphere of the unit to cater for some of those pupils for whom school proves to be a failure.

Notes

1 W. B. Seaver (1973) showed how the performance of younger siblings was affected by teacher expectancies based on the previous performance of an older sibling for the same teacher. Where the teacher held a negative expectancy the results showed the younger sibling to perform poorly but, where the expectancy was positive, the younger sibling performed better compared with the control group.

2 cf. A study of disruptive behaviour in one secondary school by J. Lawrence, D. Steed and P. E. Young (1978), in which they refer to what they describe as 'seasonal variations' in the reporting of disruptive behaviour by teachers.

3 The efforts made to assist Sue and others to settle in the unit were in marked contrast to the minimal efforts made by most of the secondary schools to resettle pupils returning from the unit.

4

A sanctuary for disruptive pupils

John Leavold

Over the last decade or more, successive governments in this country and the USA have offered almost parallel strategies to deal with the problems of inner city areas. In this country the response has been in the form of urban aid programmes, community development projects and the establishment of educational priority areas. The latter, part of a wider movement of compensatory education, represents an attempt to alleviate 'urban crisis' through the educational system. Reactions to these measures and to the most recent extension of this form of interventionism, the special unit movement, clearly reveals the enormous ideological gulf between those holding liberal and radical positions. However, what this ideological struggle often appears to lack is empirical foundation.

This chapter is based on a piece of research designed to supply some substance to the ideological debate concerning control and care in urban schools. The research was carried out in a large comprehensive school, referred to here as 'Downtown School', which in 1974 set up a sanctuary or unit for its problem pupils.

I began my research with several questions in mind. What was the significance of the sanctuary movement in urban working class schools? Why did this specific unit come into existence? How do the sanctuary teachers see their role? Is a radically different form of education offered? Why are pupils sent there and how do they view the sanctuary?

Downtown school: its history and environment

The school, which is officially described as comprehensive, is situated in an extremely pleasant middle/upper-class area of a London borough. However, this immediate locality provides hardly any pupils for the school, the main catchment area being outside the immediate vicinity.

The history of the school is marked by change, transition and long periods of instability. Since the details of this are relevant to the genesis of the sanctuary, Downtown's history will first be outlined before the sanctuary itself is examined.

The school was opened in June 1956 and from the beginning the number of children outstripped its facilities because of the post-war bulge in the birth rate. By 1963 the bulge had passed. The school now lost a percentage of its intake which the grammar schools, unable to accept previously, then became able to accommodate, and at the same time the first influx of immigrant children began to arrive, especially from Jamaica.

In the course of eight years, the school changed from an indigenous white to a multi-racial school. In 1971, the proportion of pupils was four immigrants to one indigenous. At about the same time a second wave of immigrants of Asian origin from either East Africa or the Indian sub-continent began to enter the school in increasing numbers. Technically, the proportion of immigrant pupils began to decline from 1971 when direct immigration from the West Indies fell away almost to nothing, but it was replaced by increasing numbers of pupils who were of West Indian extraction but had been born in the United Kingdom. In 1972, the proportion of ethnic minority pupils in the school was 54 per cent. In 1973, it was 44 per cent. This was the last official count as DES policy has now forbidden the keeping of such records. Up to 1971, the number of non-English-speaking pupils was so small that it was possible to cope with them by sending them to a language centre in the borough. But in the same year the staff were suddenly faced with approximately seventy pupils more than the language centre could accommodate. Two members of staff therefore had to be employed exclusively on the teaching of English as a foreign language. In the summer of 1973 a holding unit for Ugandan Asians closed and the school had a further intake of pupils in this category.

The above difficulties were exacerbated by several other factors. The first was accommodation: the change from a senior high school with 620 pupils to an all-through comprehensive with 1,650 clearly required additional buildings. At the time of the changeover only half of these were completed, though some temporary classrooms (huts) were provided. Further complications arose from the fact that the new school consisted of pupils and staff groups from three existing schools together with the new intake of 400 pupils from primary schools and a proportionate number of new staff. A third problem was the reorganisation of the school curriculum to accommodate the newly added 11–13 age group and to anticipate the raising of the school leaving age.

In addition to this, both staff and pupils had to accustom themselves to an organisational structure that they had never experienced before and a size of school that was bewildering to many. The school was divided into three for the purposes of administration and pastoral care: the lower school (years 1 and 2), the middle school (years 3 and 4) and the upper school (years 5, 6 and 7). Each school had a head, together with an assistant of the opposite sex. There were seventeen subject departments.

The inherent difficulties of the school were soon to be increased by staffing problems. Throughout 1973 staff shortages became apparent and by September 1974 the school was short of more than thirty teachers while approximately thirty were probationers. There was over a 30 per cent teacher turnover rate at that time. Part-time education was introduced which meant a four-day week for most of the children.

By 1975 the school's catchment area had become relatively stable. Large numbers of whites had moved out altogether, leaving what many staff referred to as a black ghetto. A very small number of middle class children came from outside the area, but the majority of the families lived in terraced houses, usually sharing with another family. Council property was considered a luxury available only to a few. In many homes both parents worked irregular hours, unless unemployed or sick, usually in service industries or in two local food factories.

Academic results at Downtown were poor and a very large number of children, according to the head of the compensatory department, had 'specific learning difficulties'. A huge number had low reading ages and the EFL teachers were catering for 120 pupils.

The school had changed from being the 'most popular school in the borough' in the late 1950s and early 1960s to a 'sink' school in the early and mid-1970s.

Clearly, by the spring term of 1974 Downtown was undergoing a crisis. It was during this period that the staff requested that the Director of Education should come and discuss problems which were affecting both the education of the pupils and their own health.

At this meeting it became clear that no one had any policy to deal with the crisis. However, one member of staff suggested that a 'sanctuary' might be the answer, and in this almost haphazard way the idea of a sanctuary was accepted, although few of the staff had even heard of sanctuaries. In a later interview, the Director of Education frankly admitted that he had little idea at that time of what a sanctuary was. The suggestion was seized upon because no one had anything more positive to offer.

The sanctuarians

When the sanctuary first opened the headmaster and his staff saw it as catering in the main for the type of pupil they termed a disrupter. However, it was also felt to be of value in attracting back pupils who failed to attend school regularly, for a variety of reasons, and who were loosely referred to as 'phobics'.

Despite the fact that these two blanket terms clearly mask a variety of behavioural difficulties, they have remained very much in official use as explanations of the type of problem child for whom the sanctuary best caters. From interviews with sanctuary staff, pupils, representatives of external agencies and from observations, I feel one can point to four distinct categories of pupil: disrupters, maladjusted or disturbed, school phobics and school refusers. These describe more accurately certain *regular* forms of behaviour, usually subsumed under the loose terms 'disrupter' or 'phobic'.

1 Disrupters

By far the largest proportion of children sent to the sanctuary tended to be given a diffuse label such as disrupter, trouble-maker or problem. Sometimes the disruption had followed a pattern of similar acts, occasionally of an aggressive nature, but usually the disrupter had committed a variety of misdemeanours, which Hargreaves (1975) aptly describes as 'variegated deviancy'.

2 Maladjusted or disturbed

Although there is a tendency to 'over-psychologise' in schools, there is at least a small number of children who might be regarded as disturbed. The sanctuary has in fact never been without a child clinically diagnosed or maladjusted. Once academic staff realise they cannot cope with these pupils, whom they tend to typify as strange, odd, disturbed or mental, sometimes even mad, the pastoral teachers are usually put under severe pressure to do something about them, preferably to refer them to outside agencies. Two insurmountable problems exist, however. Firstly a child cannot be referred without parental permission, which is not always forthcoming, or can take months to acquire, and secondly, in the inner urban areas especially there are huge waiting lists for assessments by educational psychologists. Therefore, as the pastoral deputy pointed out

> 'Any benefits to come out of child guidance are going to take six months to materialise. So in effect child guidance might solve the long term problems of the kids but in no way are they going to give us solutions to our short-term difficulties.'

The sanctuary thus often acts as a holding centre for such pupils. A typical case was a boy who could not be contained at the main school and spent months at the sanctuary awaiting placement in an assessment centre. He is now in a residential home described as 'a controlled environment for disturbed boys'.

3 School phobics
Whilst several pastoral heads applied the term phobic correctly – to those who *feared* school in some sense or other – it was used by a number of teachers to refer to any non-attender. Through the years, a number of phobics have attended the sanctuary regularly. It was sometimes difficult to ascertain precisely what they *feared*, but often it was the size or noise of the school; or perhaps they were unable to cope with room changes or were actually afraid of other pupils or certain teachers. There were two phobics present at the sanctuary during the period of observation.

4 School refusers
The 'school refuser' was usually typified as a 'truant' or, wrongly, as 'phobic'. The sanctuary housed not only pupils who feared school, but also those who simply *disliked* it. As with the 'phobic', it could be size, the staff, the curriculum, or the bureaucratic complexities, but it was a *dislike* not a fear. The 'refuser' was normally a far less anxious or nervous sort of pupil, and often an extrovert.

It is important to note that though the above pupils exhibited divergent forms of behaviour, they had all acquired *stabilised deviant identities* in school. To become a sanctuarian one had clearly to have passed the level of routine deviance reached through 'the rapid processing by the teacher of common and minor breaches of rules' (Hargreaves 1975). They had reached the stage where their deviant conduct was seen as a relatively permanent and central feature and was in fact considered to be 'irremediable as far as school was concerned'. In other words, both short- and long-term measures had failed to remedy the deviant behaviour. The point had also been reached where all strategies at the teachers' disposal to deal with such pupils, whether 'disrupters', 'maladjusted', 'school phobics' or 'school refusers', had been exhausted. As one year head stated, 'You know as well as I do that you run a list of sanctions and when they've all run out you've got problems.'

Once the typification had become stabilised the only thing that could change it was a different form of behaviour over a long period. If more acceptable behaviour was shown, however, there was a tendency for it to be explained away as 'superficial' or 'ephemeral'. Any 'type transformation' was therefore unlikely as long as pupils remained at school. At this point the pupil was usually handled by a senior member of staff and as the pastoral deputy head pointed out, 'Once their good offices failed, one usually had a classic case for sanctuary treatment.'

When this point was reached the usual practice was for the deputy head to call a case conference attended by the appropriate head of school, head of year and teacher in charge of the sanctuary and if after discussion there was general agreement that the child should go to the sanctuary, the parents were summoned. No parents had ever refused to let their children be sent there, which is perhaps understandable since exclusion was the likely alternative. The pupil was then usually sent for and advised that he or she would gain from a period at the sanctuary and it was always stressed that it was not a punishment. Nevertheless, most went reluctantly, although after a very short period most seemed to lose any desire to return to the main school.

The sanctuary – physical structure

The sanctuary is situated approximately a quarter of a mile from the main school, in a deconsecrated church built in 1890. In the evenings part of the building is used by a youth club and in the mornings a small play group occupies the ground floor hall. The main sanctuary area is on the second floor and comprises two rooms in rather dilapidated condition. The larger, approximately 30 by 20 feet, is used for the day-to-day work. The walls have been decorated by staff and pupils and there are good storage cupboards, tables and chairs. The second room, measuring roughly 15 by 20 feet and requiring lighting throughout the year, has a direct outside telephone line, and is used for a variety of purposes, such as interviewing pupils and parents, isolating 'difficult' pupils, and also for entertaining the many visitors to the sanctuary. On the same floor is a large hall which until pronounced a fire risk was used for badminton and volleyball. On the ground floor the staff and pupils have access to a kitchen complete with cooker, fridge and hot water and to the large hall for recreation when it is vacated by the play group at twelve noon each day.

These facilities and the size of the pupil group (usually no more than twelve) give the three sanctuary staff a flexibility much harder to achieve in a school of 1,600 pupils. All the bureaucratic procedures necessary for the functioning of a large comprehensive school are dispensed with, as are the legacies of the public school system still popular in many comprehensives, such as morning prayers, prefect systems and competition, sporting or academic. Registration periods are not required, for the register can be marked at a glance, or weekly, as is the usual practice.

In contrast to Keddie (1971) who found significant contradictions and ambiguities between teachers' stated intentions and their practices, the researcher found a marked congruence between the sanctuary teachers' descriptions of their methods and procedures when interviewed and what was actually observed. The flexible arrangements and individual care and attention which they stressed were realised in practice and formed the most striking characteristic of the sanctuary. For example, there was a time-table for academic mornings and recreational afternoons, but it could be, and often was, disregarded without the unthinkable repercussions that such action would have caused at the main school. If a group was highly motivated as they often were, the pupils could be allowed to carry on their work into another subject period. An individual child who had reached a crucial stage of his work – perhaps a painting or piece of writing – was invariably allowed to continue. Children did not have to carry complex individual time-tables with them. There were thus no bells, no groups waiting to enter, no areas having to be vacated, except for internal arrangements, and no teachers having to suddenly depart for lessons elsewhere. They could, and often did, 'down tools' and go into the park or to the canal if it was a nice day, or to the museum to see something they had just been discussing in history, without any worry about cover, permission or form filling. Breaks could be, and often were, taken at any time and on an individual basis if necessary. At only one time in the sanctuary day was an absolute halt imperative, and that was at 11.30 a.m. when most people had to leave to fall in with the main school lunch programme.

In addition, the sanctuary staff could and did give pupils individual attention in every lesson, and when a child with a specific difficulty needed a morning or a day's help to be got over a particular hurdle, this was possible, for it was very easy for the time to be made up with the other pupils over the following few days.

Although the sanctuary teachers certainly lacked specialist teaching skills and advanced visual aids and equipment, they had at their disposal perhaps a more important commodity for which many main school staff would have traded their video machines, namely the availability at the same time of three separate teaching areas, two adjacent and one downstairs. The sanctuary staff could therefore split their already small group, placing the pupils in different rooms according to behavioural or academic criteria. An individual who seriously misbehaved could be isolated with one or two teachers if necessary, as in the case of a maladjusted child, without any break in the flow of the lesson. These other areas were sometimes used for vocational and personal counselling. If a child did come to school with a serious problem one teacher could be released to go to the home or social services office or use the telephone (a facility to which many main school staff had little access). A child who had not arrived could be looked for in the well known meeting spots of the locality if it was thought necessary.

Being off-site gave even greater flexibility to the sanctuary staff. For instance, they could allow smoking and the wearing of casual clothes, which would have been difficult to accommodate had the sanctuary been located in the school grounds. On the other hand, the actual structure of the building, as the staff pointed out, lent itself to much greater control. There were no corridors to chase around in, no real hiding places, no problem of movement, and no matter how the pupils were grouped or sub-divided, they were always readily accessible. It was undoubtedly the most highly controlled area of the school.

Social relationships

It is not difficult to imagine how social relationships are affected in large urban schools undergoing or just emerging from the sort of crisis examined earlier, where there are problems of accom-modation, staff shortage, rapid turnover and a changing popu-lation. The tendency will be for the development of neutral, contractual (or formal) and impersonal relationships. The school at that time had 108 staff and 1,600 pupils, and it seemed to the observer that whatever sub-divisions were introduced to combat the danger of anonymity, teachers were still unable to develop meaningful relationships with the majority of pupils. The poss-ible exception would be a year head who stayed at the lower end of the school for a long period. The dilemma was that teachers taught either a small number of classes all the time, and therefore knew few other children, or a larger cross-section with whom they developed a rather superficial relationship, which still nevertheless constituted only a small percentage of the 1,600. Yet as pupils had access to *all* areas of the school, teachers were expected to carry out various duties facing large numbers of children whose names they often never knew. They had little time to build up meaningful relationships or discuss curricula or any-thing outside normal routine matters.

The academic and pastoral sub-divisions also influenced social relationships, leading at times to animosity between two sets of teachers. There was a tendency for the 'academics' to insist on dealing with only the academic difficulties of the children and the pastoral with their personal problems, pupils being pushed from one to the other. In three years at Downtown there were meetings and bitter arguments to decide which teachers should deal with which aspects of a child's education. This issue was never fully resolved and as a result staff appeared to become even more formal with each other and pupils.

The sanctuary lent itself to the development of quite different social relationships. While teachers there obviously had their difficult moments they did not suffer, as did the main school staff, from that total immersion in the procedures of the large school which made merely getting through the day a task in itself.

Relationships at the sanctuary tended to be more effective, not typified by the impersonality or formality of the main school. Together virtually all day, teachers and pupils shared most things. There was, for example, no separate staffroom or toilet, although these could have been easily created. All breaks were taken together, coffee or tea made sometimes by staff, sometimes by pupils, and cigarettes and sweets shared. Lunch was taken together by those who stayed (the majority), and afterwards staff and pupils invariably spent the rest of the lunch hour together. Jokes and verbal back-chat were exchanged quite readily as long as remarks did not become personal. The pupils nevertheless respected the sanctuary teachers, but as teachers of a different sort. There was a sense of community, almost of family, something noticed by nearly all visitors and by all the teachers who taught there. The sanctuarians themselves were very possessive about this tightly knit community; visitors were looked upon very suspiciously and teachers from the main school had to serve something of a probationary period before being accepted, if at all. When misbehaviour did occur there was sometimes a threat of removal of privileges, but in general punishments of a retributive nature were avoided in favour of counselling.

A striking feature of the sanctuary teachers was their attitude to their pupils, characterised by dedication, genuine caring friendship, understanding and a willingness to work beyond the call of duty. In addition to giving up lunch hours and breaks (something which few staff at the main school even considered), nothing appeared too much for the staff to do in order to help the sanctuarians, whether it was losing a game of draughts on purpose to give encouragement, helping with an academic problem or making arrangements to alleviate home difficulties. On occasions the teachers had taken children home when they had nowhere to go, and had even provided clothes and food. The teachers, who regarded themselves as a team, had occasionally spent their own money providing articles of furniture for the sanctuary itself. They had regularly tramped the streets in search of a child. There was certainly no academic-pastoral division there.

Understandably, many of the sanctuarians developed a close friendship with the staff. Virtually every week ex-sanctuarians were in touch to tell them what they were doing and asking when they could come in. One West Indian girl who had left over two years ago rang weekly. It seemed the sanctuary staff were the only real friends she had.

The inter-pupil relationships also seemed to contain less violence and aggression than those in the main school. The group, consisting of pupils from the third, fourth, fifth and sixth years, was the most comprehensive in the school racially and intellectually, containing roughly equal numbers of black and white children, and pupils ranging from GCE to bordering on ESN standard. And although some obviously had particular friends they appeared to mix well and there was a marked absence of vandalism.

Intimate knowledge

The advantages inherent in the structure of the sanctuary and the development of close social relationships enabled the staff to acquire an intimate knowledge of their pupils. Any educationalist who visited the sanctuary would have recognised immediately a clear manifestation of the pastoral care system, and with the permanent availability of a telephone, the sanctuary teachers appeared to have developed to the full every standard pastoral care technique and procedure. In addition to their own counselling they not only liaised closely with every relevant external agency, but were also personally acquainted with many of their representatives. As regards teacher–parent contact, it is difficult to visualise closer relationships, for the sanctuary teachers regularly visited their pupils' homes.

The sanctuary teachers also had a thorough knowledge of the community itself, especially the popular haunts where pupils were likely to be found if not at school, such as the local park, library or certain derelict houses. They knew many people associated with these areas, such as the local café owner, for example, who was a constant source of information about the whereabouts and behaviour of children.

Whereas the teachers of the main school often acquired only surface knowledge of their pupils, the sanctuary teachers, through constant observation and social interaction, were able to build up personal profiles of each child which included information that their former pastoral heads at the main school had no knowledge of.

However, as Bernstein (1971 and 1975) succinctly points out in his work on 'classification and framing' and 'visible and invisible pedagogies', approaches that encourage more of the individual to be made public or visible, such as his or her thoughts, failings and values, paradoxically expose that individual to the possibility of not only greater care, but also of greater control. As a result, socialisation, for example, could be more intensive or more penetrating. During my period of observation at the sanctuary I saw this 'intimate knowledge' clearly used for purposes of both care and control.

Detailed knowledge of background difficulties and emotional problems certainly enabled the sanctuary staff to intervene to *help* pupils or advise parents or guardians. Allowances were regularly made for children who were known to be undergoing personal problems. The sanctuary teachers usually knew when and when not to press things, avoiding unnecessary explosive situations. One of the West Indian girls, for example, was allowed to arrive at least an hour late every morning, because the teachers realised that before she left the house she had to cook, clean and wash for her father and five brothers and sisters whilst her mother served a year's jail sentence. She was even allowed to sleep for an hour or so at the sanctuary if necessary before commencing lessons. In addition, 'intimate knowledge' of a child's past school experiences often resulted in the staff's modifying their approach to a particular pupil. A boy who, it was discovered, had developed almost a phobia about maths because he had been ridiculed by a maths teacher in front of the class, was given extra care and understanding in an effort to regenerate his self-confidence in that subject. Numerous examples of this 'intimate knowledge' used as a means of caring could be cited.

However, the researcher found the use of 'intimate knowledge' as a control device in the sanctuary more problematic. The term 'control' is used in two different ways. First in a technical organisational sense, referring to the clearly visible means of maintaining social order which any social formation must have. Recently the more radical writers use the concept more in terms of 'deep structure', that is, control as the imposition of meaning, implying a notion of one order attempting to dominate and control another.

Undoubtedly, the use of 'intimate knowledge' by the sanctuary staff as a means of control in the former 'surface' sense, relating to behaviour, punctuality and attendance, was clearly in evidence. It was, for example, difficult for a sanctuarian to put a foot anywhere in the locality during school time without being seen by one of the staff's contacts. Also apparent was the fact that both teachers seemed to know the most vulnerable aspect of each child. On a number of occasions one teacher would continually telephone a boy who liked staying in bed, knowing that although he wasn't answering, he would eventually have had enough and come to school. Another example was the sanctuary staff's use of their knowledge of a boy's Rastafarian commitment to help them control him, for on several occasions when his behaviour was anti-social I heard them remind him of the love and peace aspects of his convictions. At other times and with other pupils it might be a word to a parent, another relation or a particular social worker, a threat of no table-tennis, talk of a home visit, something which the sanctuary teachers *knew* to be particularly meaningful to that individual, which would have the desired effect. This surface form of control was thus clearly visible.

It was extremely difficult to reach any real conclusions regarding control in the sense of 'deep' structure. However, the observations on curricula and pedagogy in the next section seem relevant to this issue.

Pedagogy

The teaching situation at the sanctuary was very interesting as it contained elements of traditionalism compounded with features of progressivism. Although the group was split up on occasions, for example when some older pupils took CSE history or when slow readers were withdrawn, the sanctuarians were mostly taught together in the main room. A few tables were grouped together to form a large oblong surface around which the pupils were seated with the teachers among them. It was a mixed ability grouping, which had been adopted not because the teachers were firm believers in this approach, but because the teacher–pupil ratio and the make-up of the group lent themselves to this.

Inevitably the children worked very much at their own level. The lessons were characterised as much as any other part of the day by the more symmetrical teacher–pupil relationships and by informality, so much so that the transition from break to lesson and vice versa was not always apparent. Once the teacher had introduced a lesson, work began with the teachers moving about and helping individuals. Encouraged by the actual classroom organisation, pupils were allowed to talk about work or other interests, sometimes exchanging the odd pleasantry with the staff; they were also allowed to eat, chew or even smoke. A child could also get up, move around, or go to the cupboard or to the toilet without having to ask permission. However, it was a situation of freedom not licence. The flow of the lesson rarely stopped. If someone became too rowdy or got out of control, as did a maladjusted girl on occasions, he or she would simply be told to get on, but if that failed the offender would probably be moved to another room. When I questioned one of the sanctuary teachers about this, he said that it had just 'come about', and it seemed to me, as an observer, that it was probably the result of some sort of covert teacher–pupil negotiations, for some of the sanctuarians had certainly indicated to me that they would not have tolerated a more formal approach. Nevertheless, the blackboard was used fairly regularly in the conventional teaching manner.

However, this was about as far as the symmetry between teacher and pupil went in the pedagogical relationship because in terms of the knowledge transmitted, the relationship was unquestionably asymmetrical. Despite all their criticisms of the main school, the sanctuary teachers had never seriously attacked the vital centre of the system, the curriculum. They saw the curriculum as most other teachers seem to, as neutral, as given.

The curriculum offered at the sanctuary was a traditional one. Although the sanctuarians received an enormous amount of indidivual attention and were given graded work to suit their different ages and abilities, it was from textbooks designed specifically for mixed-ability classes – books and materials geared strongly to separate disciplines, such as geography, history, art, drama, English and maths. There was no move towards subject integration and even when CSE courses were offered the teachers had made no attempt to write their own Mode 3 syllabuses, but accepted either the main school recommendations or the official examining board syllabus. Numerous opportunities in this area in terms of local geography and history had been disregarded in favour of world wars, the Danish dairy industry etc. There had been an attempt at some Black Studies but it had been dropped because it was felt the children were 'uninterested', and although one sanctuary teacher shared an interest in the pop world with several of the boys, this remained a means of communication, an interest outside the curriculum. Some pupils painted and drew pop stars, but the only legitimate knowledge in terms of work, in terms of exams, was 'expert' knowledge (see Keddie 1971), and there was little attempt to legitimate the commonsense world of the pupils.

One might wonder why at the sanctuary – an ideal context for pedagogic innovation – such change had not come about. The crucial question here appears to be teacher consciousness and the social and ideological influences which affect this. It was an example of the way in which the teachers' training had pre-dated much of the recent discussion in the sociology of knowledge about the relativity of knowledge or the class-based nature of knowledge. It had also pre-dated more recent discussions about different modes of pedagogy, particularly Freire's notions on conscientisation (1972) which have achieved circulation amongst younger teachers.

The pedagogical approach at Downtown sanctuary did, nevertheless, point to something of significance, namely that the marriage of a small teacher–pupil ratio and more symmetrical pupil–teacher social relationships appeared to create a climate conducive to the ready acceptance of 'expert' knowledge by working-class children. Although there was no hard evidence except for improved attendance figures for 'school phobics' and 'school refusers', there was unanimous agreement amongst staff and main school staff that the pupils generally worked harder, produced more work and had, in some cases, made dramatic academic improvements.

Identity

One of the central concerns in this study was to consider the effect of sanctuary attendance on pupil identity: whether attendance encouraged the internalisation of the deviant labels that pupils arrived with or increased the possibility of 'type transformation' – in other words, whether the pupils to whom the label 'deviant' had been attached came to see themselves in terms of the label. Having observed several sanctuarians arrive, it seemed to me initially that whether sent for non-attendance or disruption the pupils experienced in Goffman's terms (1963), a sense of stigma about being attached to the sanctuary. During the first few days, although pupils were often surprised to see a fairly structured work situation, having often been informed otherwise, they usually wanted to return to the main school, feeling that the sanctuary was some kind of punishment area. However, these sentiments tended to dissipate very quickly after a week or so. During my entire period of observation I found only one pupil persisting in a wish to go back to the main school.

There were undoubtedly a number of factors which could have

encouraged the internalisation of a deviant identity. These influences all appeared to be outside the sanctuary, such as the hostile, pejorative statements of a small number of teachers made to the pupils when they passed through the school on their way to lunch; the refusal of many of their peers to believe that there really existed a structured working environment at the sanctuary; and the questioning, concerned response when they told a stranger or relative where they went to school. However, as was revealed in interviews with the sanctuarians, they seemed to have no sense of guilt or of being in a punishment area, but spoke with confidence about the present and the future. It was also noticeable that whenever anyone did attempt to undermine the sanctuary, the pupils showed a great willingness to argue to the contrary and were not ashamed to say where they went to school. The reason for this attitude appeared to be very much related to the social world of the sanctuary itself. Their experiences there seem to have outweighed possible negative external influences on identity formation.

The sanctuary to them was quite obviously 'school' and it compared very favourably with the main school. The sanctuary, it was considered, did everything the main school did, and better. They were 'understood', 'listened to', treated 'more like adults', did 'more work', received a superior form of teaching and were able in many cases to prepare for examinations which they would never have expected to take. In addition, initially dubious parents generally became very supportive of the sanctuary. For most of the sanctuarians Downtown was a place with poor teachers, who made little effort to teach or to understand them, a place where you could easily get away with things, and which was more likely to lead to the dole than university. If anything was considered deviant, it was the school. The sanctuarians had no sense of being excluded and in general they had no aspirations to return to the main school.

There was little evidence of social stratification at the sanctuary. Teachers rarely adopted the labels the pupils arrived with except for the maladjusted girl with whom they had great difficulty in coping, who was therefore considered to have had her problems correctly diagnosed. Most of the labels the pupils had acquired at the main school were rapidly forgotten because most of the sanctuarians did not behave in a manner that corresponded to such labels. For example, the school refusers and school phobics virtually all became regular attenders and the so called disrupters were certainly far less disruptive. It was only the rare pupil who could not in some sense be resocialised. Whereas at the main school overt labelling by teachers was rife, it was distinctly lacking at the sanctuary.

Unlike pupils at the main school, therefore, who had acquired a stabilised deviant identity, the sanctuarians had an opportunity to negotiate or renegotiate theirs, and from my observations most had been successful in doing so and had undergone or were undergoing 'type transformation', more difficult to achieve in the main school. In the sanctuary the staff had had time to build up an 'intimate knowledge' of pupils and the pupils had the opportunity for negotiation. When asked what a child was like, the sanctuary staff offered a detailed profile as opposed to one all-encompassing label, which I found to be the usual practice at the main school where working conditions were less favourable. The sanctuary teachers regularly mentioned facets of a child's character and intellectual capacity or something which had not been known generally at the main school, where he or she was often identified as merely a 'disrupter' or 'phobic'. If there was a tendency at all in terms of labelling, it was towards 'soft' academic labels, for with most of the sanctuarians now conforming, the necessity for social/behavioural labels had mostly disappeared. Occasionally amongst themselves the staff used labels such as 'slow' or 'lazy'. However, whilst a number of studies seem to suggest that such labels would imply low expectations of a child, the sanctuary teachers seemed to react in the opposite fashion, launching themselves into a policy of positive discrimination to lift the child out of this position.

Conclusion

The main objective of this study was to focus on one specific sanctuary in order to give some substance to the ideological debate about special units. But whereas it is comparatively simple at the level of ideology or theory to present ideas in relatively clear-cut forms, once one becomes involved in empirical analysis one finds that social practice is never as straightforward as ideological or theoretical forms would have it. This is evident in the care/control debate, central to this study. It is quite reasonable, for example, to see sanctuaries in the context of the history and contemporary development of urban working class education as another control device for coping with the disruptive urban population. On the other hand, the sanctuary can be seen in liberal terms as a very different type of educational experience. However, any simplistic characterisation of sanctuaries as either controlling or caring mechanisms does not do full justice to the phenomenon. This research has shown that principles of care and principles of control are inextricably linked, and the 'intimate knowledge' of pupils which is acquired in the sanctuary makes it possible for the teacher either to help pupils to become much more autonomous, liberated, critically-minded persons, or to integrate with the existing social order.

One is therefore logically brought back to the crucial element, the consciousness and the ideology of the central agents of the process – the teachers. Whatever educational contexts are created (theoretically one could create sanctuary conditions in a school in terms of ratios, use of space and relationships), what is realised in these situations depends on the consciousness of the teachers working within them. In other words, if the models of society that most teachers have in their consciousness are not substantially changed, if teachers still hold very conservative or hierarchical models, then inevitably these relationships, this 'intimate knowledge' will be used not for purposes of radically transforming anything but for reproducing 'the system' as it is.

What this study has suggested is that out of urban educational crisis has emerged the potential for changing the values and principles embodied in state education. Even though Downtown sanctuary was very much a reproducer of 'the system', its teacher–pupil ratio, pedagogical possibilities, social relationships and apparent success with pupils considered uncontainable, have brought into question the way in which large comprehensive schools are functioning. Throughout the entire period of observation, both teachers and pupils continually questioned the viability of the very large school such as Downtown in which it seems barely possible to foster sound social relationships or to acquire the sort of 'intimate knowledge' which will enable teachers to respond more sensitively and effectively to the needs of their problem pupils. Beneath this issue lies a more fundamental question which a single case study such as this can do no more than reassert: where does the problem really lie? Within the sanctuarians and the sanctuary, within the schools, as currently constituted, or within the wider social framework?

5
Developing a policy for a support unit
Terry Emerson

The North Camden Schools' Support Unit was established in March 1979 under the auspices of the Inner London Education Authority's 'Disruptive Pupils Scheme'. It was initially envisaged that the unit would serve four secondary comprehensive schools in the north of the London borough of Camden. The consortium of four schools comprised one mixed-sex, two girls' and one boys' school, together numbering a roll of approximately 3,000. Based on this figure the unit was to have three staff and a capacity of eighteen pupils, giving a teacher/pupil ratio of 1:6. In 1981, the consortium was increased to five on the addition of a further mixed comprehensive secondary school. A further member of staff was added and the pupil capacity became twenty-four, preserving the staff/pupil ratio. It was to cater mainly for fourth- and fifth-year pupils as on-site behavioural units existed or were being planned for lower years.

I have been asked to describe the way in which the staff appointed to the unit gradually developed a policy. The foundations for this were provided in the authority-wide scheme for disruptive pupils, but since 1979 an individual character has been superimposed upon this through the interaction of local conditions, the convictions and the attributes of the staff, and experience gained through the day-to-day running of the unit. The major features of the policy—referral, reintegration, the curriculum and the rules system – will be explained, but first some further background to the policy-making process will be set out.

Accommodation was found in the very heart of London some two to five miles distant from individual schools but well served by public transport. The premises chosen already housed an evening youth club funded by a long established educational trust. This was to prove a great advantage as it presented us with a readily available source of knowledge of the local environment, its inhabitants and the economic and social problems. Also the youth club already catered for many of the pupils who attended the consortium schools and staff links were soon forged.

We spent a whole academic term studying the needs of the schools, the pupils and the exact requirements of the LEA scheme under which we had been created. Our next task, we knew, would be to evolve academic, behavioural and management structures appropriate to our task, then to win acceptance of these and publicise them. Despite the immediate needs of the schools and other pressures, this planning time was granted. Indeed, much of whatever success we have been credited with has stemmed from this vital and essential period of time. With hindsight, it would appear such time is perhaps the first priority of any relatively new scheme and certainly should be considered a valid prerequisite of both off- and on-site educational units.

The first study we undertook examined our role as broadly defined in the ILEA policy document and compared this with the requirements of the schools. There immediately arose a number of issues which could have caused a clash of objectives and it became clear that our final policies would essentially be a compromise between the policy document and the schools' requirements. But the ILEA policy document set out some principles which we found we could adopt:

1 The unit's management structure was to be composed of the teacher-in-charge, school heads, ILEA divisional representatives and other such seconded advisory expertise as we deemed necessary. (We decided to add a senior pupil to this.)
2 The unit was clearly to be an annexe of the consortium schools.
3 Finance, with the exception of teachers' salaries, rent and other administrative costs, was to be the responsibility of the consortium schools. (It was later settled that each school would contribute funds on an equal share of costs basis and not by the number of pupils they referred, as with many schemes.)
4 Referred pupils would remain on roll in the parent school whilst attending the unit.
5 Referred pupils should generally not include those deemed 'clinically maladjusted', 'chronic truants', or any deemed as needing other forms of special education.

6 The unit's primary purpose would be whenever possible to reintegrate its pupils into mainstream secondary education.

To these basic guidelines we added a number of specific goals of our own. These were:

1 To recognise the placing of fifth-year pupils into employment or further education as a valid form of 'reintegration'.
2 To set clear academic as well as behavioural goals for all pupils whatever their current level of achievement at the time of referral.
3 To guide and assist pupils in the development of self-control without the use of punitive discipline or other conditioning techniques. The approach was to be one which sought to maximise the pupils' co-operation and understanding.
4 To become a natural extension of each school's pastoral system, despite their own very different structures and approaches.
5 To stimulate pupils' interest in further education and training possibilities.
6 To promote, encourage and emphasise each pupil's positive skills as well as illustrating the behavioural skills they lacked.

Having completed this first stage, we felt the need to make ourselves and our purpose widely known to the teaching staff of the consortium schools. To achieve this, the unit staff spent a great deal of time in each school throughout the summer term of 1979. Many useful contacts were made which would not have been possible without this setting-up period.

Yet another major area of study was the nature and organisation of the support agencies available to the unit. We wished to draw into the scheme not only agencies already provided for our support by the ILEA, but also local social services, police and voluntary bodies who had, or were likely to have, a good knowledge of our future pupils. In the course of this we made ourselves known to traders, businesses and individuals in the local community who might be of help. This was later to assist us greatly when it came to monitoring our pupils' behaviour out of school. The knowledge gained also gave us a better perspective on the pupils' future employment prospects, the size and nature of local amenities and the social and economic deprivations that existed. In short, we gained some vital insights which would help us to appreciate the current lifestyle of our pupils, their future hopes and likely frustrations.

Having completed our initial period of study we needed to consider the advantages and disadvantages of our somewhat spartan accommodation. There was a limited number of rooms and this would, we knew, help us in the control of pupil movement and in maintaining order, while their spaciousness meant there would be no overcrowding. The academic curriculum was going to be restricted by the building as it lacked security, storage space and facilities for the sciences and arts and crafts. Although some of these shortcomings would in time be compensated for, initially pupils would need to be taken back to their parent schools for some subjects. This, we thought, would give extra motivation for a return to mainstream schooling. The greatest of the building's advantages lay in its central location near to inner London's wealth of educational facilities. Additionally, the premises possessed much sporting and leisure equipment which was available for our use.

The staff appointed to the unit were as carefully selected as our site. Experience had suggested that the most important qualities would be firstly, strength of character and charisma on which much discipline is based and, secondly, the ability and motivation to research and teach literally any subjects. In the event a careful balance of additional skills has been kept and subject advisers are available to assist and provide in-service training.

In evolving basic policy we identified a number of behavioural qualities that staff would need to demonstrate. These could be described as a professional, strict but caring approach to the pupils and their problems; honesty, especially when discussing pupils amongst themselves and with the pupils and their families; a direct but tactful approach in expressing our views to all; an openness to admitting mistakes and accepting criticisms from whatever source; and finally, whenever possible, consistency in our dealings with everyone.

Referral system

Perhaps the most important of all areas in our policy planning was the referral system. We realised that at no other time would so many people be involved with a given pupil and it would be at this stage that we would make the crucial first contact with those concerned. We knew that all future relationships, progress and possibly our ultimate success, would depend on this process working both speedily and efficiently.

In building the policy we had to consider the needs of the schools, the pupils and parents, the information which the unit staff would need to collate and, to a lesser extent, the interests of the support services. The schools clearly requested that the process should be a speedy one, yet we and our support services would need time to collect and consider information, to make home visits and to perform the many additional administrative tasks. We anticipated that the pupils and their families might well be emotionally stressed at this time. Here we would need to allay fears and gain their confidence, all without unduly prolonging the process of referral or placing extra strain upon the family, which might already be in considerable disarray.

In an attempt to make the referral process as speedy as possible, we decided to give it the highest priority. In practical terms this has meant, when necessary, dropping other work. We decided to make home visits about referrals at any time convenient to the family, which in practice meant much evening and weekend work. The effect of these measures has been to give an average referral time of only four to seven working days from the moment we receive the completed referral form.

A difficulty in the referral process, which we clearly foresaw, was the need to be absolutely impartial over any dispute between schools and parents: we could not act as arbitrators or sit in judgement. Both we and the schools took the view that the unit was an extension of each school's pastoral system, an attempt to keep a pupil within normal full-time education. It was decided that when a pupil or a parent rejected placement in the unit, the pupil would not be required to attend; in the event we have had only one refusal to date.

In the planning stage we recognised that the assembling of information on the pupils raised some sensitive issues. Such information would need to be collected speedily, should contain neither supposition nor rumour, and should not infringe the privacy of a pupil's family. We decided to allow all records, assessments and written statements concerning pupils to be open to scrutiny by both the pupil and parents. We felt that we should not record anything which we could not stand by. (Our current open record policy applies only to those papers of which unit staff are the sole authors and not to papers or records written by others which are not kept in the unit.) The object of this policy was to promote confidence in us, encourage frankness and honest evaluations between ourselves and the family concerned.

The referral system was broken down into three clear parts, each of these a reflection of particular aims and objectives. Stage one is carried out by the parent school. The year tutor obtains the head's permission to refer (often after a long review), alerts the educational welfare officer, ascertains from the unit that a vacancy exists and then seeks an interview with the pupil's parents. The only action taken by the unit at this stage is to alert our own education welfare officer to the possibility of a referral and to start the collation of background data if the family agrees.

Stage two is the initial review process undertaken at first by the unit, the education welfare officer and school staff. This stage does not advance further until the referral form has been received, which signifies parental approval. Then there is a meeting of all concerned; it is usually chaired by the teacher-in-charge and the parents have a right to attend.

At the meeting information regarding the pupil's problems in school is reviewed, along with any other relevant data, in order to build a profile. Confidential information is only released on a 'need to know' basis and with parental approval.

The purpose of the meeting and the profile is to assist in reaching decisions about the following:

1 Whether the referral is likely to help family, pupil and school.
2 Whether the referral could upset behavioural, academic or other balances in the unit.
3 Whether the pupil is likely to benefit academically by attending.
4 What aspirations the pupil may have in terms of qualifications and/or employment.
5 How unit staff could develop an appropriate behavioural and academic programme.
6 What alternatives are available should unit provision prove to be unsatisfactory at some future date.

The most important questions for the meeting are, of course, whether the pupil is suitable for placement and whether he or she agrees to attend. Another important function of the meeting is the choice of a 'key worker' for the pupil, often referred to by the pupils as the 'minder'. The 'key worker' system requires that one suitably qualified and knowledgeable person should co-ordinate all action to be taken outside the unit. This cuts the need for unit staff to be continually in contact with many separate individuals or agencies as well as ensuring that information reaches the correct places at the right time. It entails the formal monitoring of progress and prevents useless duplication of effort and work. From the families' point of view it reduces the number of visitors coming to discuss their children's problems and progress. Most often the 'key worker' is the education welfare officer or family social worker or, in very exceptional circumstances, a member of the unit staff.

Stage three of the referral process involves the 'key worker' and a unit staff member making a home visit. We attach a good deal of importance to this event for the following reasons:

1 It gives us a chance to meet the family in their normal environment and it also means that the parents will be more at ease and more forthcoming than if summoned to either the school or the unit.
2 It helps to show the pupil that we will have a direct line of communication to the parents.
3 We can present to the pupil and parents our methods of operation, policies and academic curriculum and discuss any special arrangements they wish to make or problems with which we might give assistance.

At the end of the home visit a date is given for the pupil's first attendance and the parents are given an open invitation to visit the unit without having to make an appointment.

Reintegration policy

As has been stated, we conceived of two main types of reintegration. One of these is direct reintegration into the adult world of employment and growing responsibilities. For this we have established links with further education establishments, leavers' courses, link courses, work experience schemes and other sources of aid and guidance. The level of success can be judged from the fact that up to the present no pupil wishing to obtain employment or further education has failed to do so.

The second type of reintegration is the return to full-time mainstream education. In our planning we set criteria for success as 'being able to complete satisfactorily and without further supervision or exclusion, the pupil's remaining time at school, no matter how long or short that may be'. About a third of pupils have attempted to reintegrate in this way and the majority have been successful. It has proved a rare occurrence, however, with fifth-year pupils, as we foresaw. Although each school in the consortium made its sixth form unconditionally available for unit pupils, only a very small number has taken advantage of this.

In anticipation of difficulties in returning pupils to the main schools, criteria were agreed in the policy planning phase to establish the pupil's readiness and determine the optimum time for transfer. The guidelines established were:

1 No pupil would be forced to return within a predetermined time limit to formal schooling.
2 Any request for reintegration would be considered at a case conference chaired by the 'keyworker' in which the pupil and parents would be encouraged to participate.
3 Account would be taken of any academic problems and of the availability in the main school of remedial support and the flexibility of time-table options.
4 Careful consideration should also be given to the pupil's present behavioural stability and its chances of surviving if full reintegration was attempted.
5 The review should also consider the stability of the pupil's home life as extreme pressures might prevent a successful return to school.
6 Any reintegration should of necessity depend on the main school's prevailing commitments. The busiest times of the year would need to be avoided and certain other factors would need to be considered. Should particular teachers with whom the pupil had formerly come into conflict be avoided? Should an attempt be made to avoid certain peers or peer groups? In practice, our policy has been always to say that such problems should not be evaded since one of the aims of the unit is to enable pupils to cope with and control their behavioural problems. It is therefore necessary for them to face their prejudices and antipathies regarding teachers, peers and academic subjects.
7 Finally, it was established that the unit should provide continuing support for reintegrated pupils. The EWOs and unit staff would keep in close contact and make regular visits to the main school, while the pupils would be permitted to visit the unit as often as they wished.

The academic programme

It was decided, with reintegration in mind, to place a relatively strong emphasis on academic commitment and work. Some observers have criticised this decision but our position is that, unlike many special units, we have not set out to provide 'alternative schooling' or 'behavioural therapy'. Our conscious intention has been to enable the referred pupils to remain within the overall influence of mainstream education despite the fact that the unit was situated at some distance from the school campus.

In designing the curriculum we had mainly to consider fourth- and fifth-year pupils, taking into account not only their needs but also those of the parent schools (including examination requirements) and potential employers. One of our basic problems was the number of referring schools, which had differing emphases and approaches, not to mention a wealth of Mode 3 CSE syllabuses. As many courses were based on a schematic or worksheet approach, few standard textbooks were available to us. Our own financial resources were finite and our most valuable resource, time, could not be stretched to allow each school's courses to be reproduced at the required level. Yet our programme had to aim at developing pupils' attainment in order to minimise any discrepancy between themselves and their peers by the time reintegration became viable. So all pupils would be required to study for at least three public examination papers at CSE or GCE O level. In the teaching of all subjects three related perspectives were to be taken into account: academic content, relevance to employment, and potential for leisure.

The subjects on the time-table were divided into compulsory and optional groups, the former occupying the mornings, the latter the afternoons. The compulsory subjects were maths, English, basic science, social studies, PE/games and careers guidance, while the optional list included art and craft, literature, microcomputing, photography, geography and history, child development, home economics and a foreign language. Substantial remedial support would be given, this being required by the majority of pupils in the unit. Additional activities would be provided at the end of the unit day when the formal curriculum work was completed. Pupils would be able to stay for extra tuition, to take part in organised games or to take advantage of the building's considerable recreational facilities, including the youth club's evening activities.

As a matter of policy, it was agreed that a written curriculum should be produced covering each subject included in the programme – a task which took two years. A postal report system has also been evolved which ensures that each week all parents receive an assessment of the work, attitude, effort and behaviour of their son or daughter. The report also contains information about punctuality and attendance.

Behavioural policy: ground rules

In the beginning it was clear that some outsiders saw the unit's function in rather simplistic terms, as changing behaviour through the application of punitive rules and harsh discipline. It was perceived as a punishment and corrective centre, a 'sin-bin' conveniently distanced from the school, where short, sharp shock methods were to be used.

Our view, based on previous experience, was that such objectives and methods did not bring about the more permanent changes in behaviour we were seeking. Our aim is to help the pupils develop techniques of self-control, thus enabling them to perform well in the absence of extrinsic punitive discipline. We believe that they should, in general, be prepared for us to be frank and honest. We try to illustrate to them the effects of their behaviour and to help them to understand the reactions of others. We also wish to show them the damage that negative behavioural responses can do to their present and future prospects, and to help them recognise and understand the individual 'triggers' which usually set their negative responses in motion. We help them to learn to control these responses and to gain enough self-confidence to face up to stressful situations successfully.

Such aims mean that each new pupil's background has to be carefully researched so that we can get as close as possible to identifying the causes of current disruptive behaviour. We accept that the unit cannot provide 'cures' for their fundamental problems. Thus our role is to help the pupils cope with the symptoms of their problems.

In practice our policy has been initially directed towards establishing good behavioural patterns in the confines of the unit, as well as developing, through academic work and social skills, each pupil's self-esteem and confidence. To do this we evolved a minimum of ground rules and settled upon an incentive system to promote their observance.

The rules were designed to encourage the pupils to attend regularly and punctually, to take responsibility for their own motivation and output, and to consider the consequences of their actions before reacting to difficult situations. The incentive system we decided to use did not involve money, tokens, food or any tangible reward but was based on the award of free time.

To implement this we shortened the school day to five hours by cutting out morning and afternoon breaks and giving pupils the choice of either a working lunch or a considerably shorter one than normal. Pupils would be required to be in attendance and ready for work at 9.30 a.m. Given positive behaviour and academic effort, a pupil could then earn sufficient free time to leave shortly after 2.30 p.m. on each working day.

Three possible forms of abuse of the free-time reward system worried us at the planning stage. What should we do about late attendance? How could we prevent a pupil returning to the parent school before the end of the school day? How would pupils spend free time out of the unit and would they disrupt the local community? To resolve the first problem we decided to insist that the pupil should make up missed time at the day's end or put in a comparable early start next day. Failure to do either would lead to the suspension of incentives for the individual concerned. To reduce the temptation to return to the parent school, we evolved a system whereby pupils wishing to do so could simply make an appointment. Failure to do this led to the withdrawal of the time incentive. Finally, to monitor the use of free time outside the unit, we decided to rely heavily on our contacts within the local community, including the police, as well as requiring pupils to account for their actions. Pupils with free time were to be encouraged to remain in the unit and could receive extra tuition or take part in other activities.

Even with this incentive policy, we felt the need for further rules to encourage good order throughout the working day. We decided to view this from an employer's point of view. A work target for the day was set in the form of a number of assignments pitched at each individual's ability level which were to be completed in tutorial groups. This system enabled us to monitor pupils' work capacity and gradually increase it as developing skills allowed. Any disruption would mean falling below the target and the subsequent loss of free time.

Finally, we decided to have what we termed an 'open door' policy. Although no pupil was to be allowed out during the minimum working day, any who felt distressed enough at any time could leave, providing they realised that they could not return. This was harsh but, we felt, realistic, and it reinforced the requirement that they should always consider the consequences of their actions.

As time, effort and output are clearly quantifiable at the end of the day, we have been able to measure performance easily and we have found that the incentive and rules system has been even more effective than we anticipated. The reaction of the pupils has been interesting and a common pattern has emerged.

Pupils at first appear to find it novel and commit themselves eagerly to earning free time. By the end of the first half-term they appear to become reluctant to leave early, instead preferring the companionship of their peers within the unit and utilising its social or academic facilities. They continue, however, to earn their time allowances and this appears to satisfy the need to have their efforts recognised as well as helping to create a positive atmosphere within the unit.

Finally, the ground rules included a requirement that pupils and staff treat each other with respect and consideration. At no stage do we as staff deny pupils the right to voice dissent or criticism. Adopting the right approach can gain them an ear and possibly a redress of any grievance, and this is part of learning a new, more positive and acceptable mode of behavioural response.

Police course

At the planning stage we looked at one further major aspect of our future pupils' likely behavioural characteristics. This was their involvement in crime and contact with the police. We estimated that over 40 per cent of our intake would, for various reasons, have fallen foul of the law and the current figure has borne out this prediction. We decided to mount a compulsory course in conjunction with the local juvenile police on aspects of criminal behaviour and the law, including consumer law. Despite some adverse comments from outside observers, we thought that regular contact between police and pupils would have two positive effects. It could lead to an improvement in attitudes towards the law and the police and could lead to the pupils' modifying their behaviour in street contact with the police.

The course candidly examines the prejudices of both the police and the pupils. It emphasises the fact that much of the pupils' view of the police and their methods is in some degree based on supposition and rumour. Specific aspects dealt with in the course include drug abuse, alcohol abuse, and common types of juvenile crime, as well as more serious crimes. All aspects of citizens' rights and those of the police are examined in detail as well as the full judicial process.

This course has two additional advantages for the pupils. Firstly, if they are subsequently involved in crime, the juvenile officers will already know them and the processes which follow may often be less difficult. Secondly, knowing the local police does mean that, if they are detained at some future time, pupils can modify their behaviour and avoid making the situation worse.

During the three years of this course, there has been a noticeable drop in the crime rate of our pupils. When pupils are taken to court a unit teacher always attends. The unit teachers have won a reputation amongst pupils, parents, police and the courts for giving honest assessments whether favourable to the pupil or not.

Conclusions

In this chapter, an attempt has been made to give an insight into how, when presented with the challenge of setting up a support unit, we attempted to define a mode of operation which would meet the needs of a consortium of inner city schools and the problem pupils of a specific community.

In a wider educational sense, the last four years have perhaps posed more questions regarding both the disruptive pupil and the provision of offsite support than we have found answers to.

The belief held by some that the schools themselves are the cause of many of our pupils' problems seems to be an over-simplification of the truth. We have observed little evidence of this; instead we might hypothesise that at a given time in a pupil's development, a school can inadvertently exacerbate into disruptive behaviour a pupil's responses to authority. The reasons why this happen are many but commonly include a growing alienation from even basic levels of academic achievement. Often pupils appear to need little except encouragement, support and a stronger sense of belonging and being needed. Many pupils feel estranged from school and perhaps lack emotional fulfilment at home. It is our belief that often the home and the family, as well as wider social and economic factors, hold the key to an individual's disruptive behaviour. If this is true, we have to ask whether schools can, given their size, organisation and academic pressures, ever realistically be expected to solve the problem of severe disruption.

A further question posed at the start of our planning concerned the relative importance of behavioural and academic goals both within the unit and in mainstream schooling. We believed then, as now, that as far as our unit was concerned, the two are of approximately equal importance. Little would have been achieved if we had simply turned out pupils with improved academic skills who proved unemployable owing to a lack of self-control. Conversely, pupils with adequate self-control are at a disadvantage unless they also possess good basic skills which will make them employable.

Another observation we would make relates to the often unco-operative relationship that exists between schools and social support services that deal directly with pupils as part of the family. We cannot blame either one side or the other, but it often seems that both parties work exclusively according to their own criteria with little attempt to understand the functions, problems and goals of the other. The result is often useless and time-consuming conflict or equally wasteful recrimination, neither of which can help the pupils or their families. Our 'keyworker' system has attempted, with some success, to overcome the barriers that exist here.

Perhaps the only true evaluation of our work will be made by the pupils themselves when they leave formal schooling and take their place in the world outside.

We can make no claim to have evolved a 'correct' set of policies applicable to all support units for disruptive pupils. Our approach relates only to a well defined set of pupils of a given age range in a specific urban location. Pupils elsewhere may have problems relating to other educational, social or environmental factors for which our approach would prove inadequate.

Note

The views expressed here should not be taken as anything but personal opinions and do not purport to represent in whole or in part the policy or views of the Inner London Education Authority.

6
Disaffected pupils in special units

Mel Lloyd-Smith

This chapter is a brief foray into the perceptions of pupils referred to special units as a result of their disruptive behaviour in school or their truancy. It is based on data from a small-scale empirical investigation carried out in four units serving comprehensive schools in a Midlands educational authority. The study attempted to describe the subjective experience of deviant pupil careers which culminated in referral to a special unit and to identify factors which were of particular salience in the perceptions of the young people concerned. The material presented here concentrates on how life in the units compared with their prior experience of school.

The four units had all developed independently; two are on-site, closed units with access confined to pupils in a single comprehensive school, while the other two are off-site, open units which accept pupils from a number of different schools. One of these is not a unit in the conventional sense, as will be shown, but represents a novel and interesting form of response to the problem of older pupils who reject or are rejected by their schools. Before the presentation of the pupil-generated data, some background details will be given of the four units to indicate their origins, organisation, aims and approach to 'treatment' and teaching.

The first of the on-site units was opened in 1976 and was situated in one of the two halls of a split-site Roman Catholic comprehensive school. Initially it was set up at the instigation of the headmaster to cater for a small group of hard-core truants to whom he applied the term 'phobics'. It was referred to, therefore, as a unit for phobics but was officially christened 'Gold' which in time became its generally accepted name. (All classes in the school are identified by the name of colours.) The head of the remedial department was given the job of setting up the unit and she recalls considerable antipathy to the idea on the part of the staff; in fact it was two years before the unit was fully accepted and receiving positive support from the teachers in general. By this time a special appointment had been made of a unit teacher and the nature of the unit had also changed. The main problem was now seen as providing adequate provision for disruptive and difficult children, since the school's policy of suspending unruly pupils had received some criticism. At the time the interviews were conducted, 'Gold' was still dealing with disruptive pupils though it had been decided that from the start of the next academic year it would become a unit for children with 'short attention spans', this had lately been perceived in the school as a problem requiring special attention.

From the start, the intention has been to foster caring and trusting relationships between staff and pupils in the unit. The pupils receive a good deal of individual attention but in addition regular group meetings are held which aim to give the pupils a greater understanding of other people's problems as well as their own. The vast majority of children in the group are subject to considerable family stress. Many are known to associate with young people who have committed offences or have themselves appeared in court.

Their behaviour when in school was in many cases characterised by hostility, shouting and swearing, and petty vandalism. It was also the case that most were low achievers in certain subjects. The unit provides individual help with English and mathematics and a range of other activities. The curriculum for fourth- and fifth-year pupils who are referred to the unit includes work experience, and this has in many cases led directly to employment after leaving school.

The other on-site unit was set up in 1978. It was created partly to meet an existing need for help for a small number of emotionally disturbed pupils and partly in anticipation of problems expected to arise from the reorganisation of two secondary high schools and one grammar school into a comprehensive federation. Initially three senior girls had exhibited problems which the staff felt might be alleviated in a school-based unit. (They were also undergoing treatment outside the school.) One girl had serious personal problems which led to disruptive behaviour in school, the second suffered a neurotic fear of the school buildings and some members of staff, and the third was traumatised by fifth-year exams; it was discovered that this girl had had learning difficulties throughout her school career but their seriousness had not been fully recognised earlier.

A number of outside experts were consulted during the early planning and they provide a certain amount of continuing support; they include a child psychiatrist, an educational welfare officer and a social worker.

The first aim of the unit was expressed as 'making the school more palatable'. Work is organised on an individual basis, the unit teacher consulting subject teachers for suggested assignments. There is some extra emphasis on craft work though in general an attempt is made to reflect the main school curriculum as closely as possible. A programme of outside visits constitutes an important element in the work of fifth-year pupils, this being part of their preparation for leaving school.

The first of the two off-site units began its life as an independent truancy centre, funded for two years by a number of trusts and since 1979 receiving financial support from the local education authority. A number of truanting secondary school pupils had begun gravitating towards a community centre whose coffee bar provided an acceptable alternative to roaming the streets. Several people connected with the centre investigated the problem of truancy locally and came to the conclusion that a need existed for an alternative form of schooling for these children. Most of the six local schools were in favour of the idea and agreement also came from the local authority and the social services department.

The project became an educational unit run by two qualified part-time teachers, open in approved cases to children who persistently truanted or who were suspended or expelled from school. Up to a total of nine pupils are accepted. Placement is usually suggested by their schools though some are initially self-referred and in all cases the referrals have to be approved by the Area Education Officer and an educational psychologist. Parents' approval must also be given and only pupils who are keen to join the unit are accepted. At present entry is restricted to those who are in the final term of their fourth year or just entering the fifth year.

Unlike many units, this one does not have the primary aim of returning its pupils to normal schooling but instead provides an alternative final year of education. The project acts, in the words of a document the teacher in charge has produced, as a half way house between school and the outside world, helping children who have seemingly reached the end of the line to build up their self-esteem, develop positive social relationships and prepare constructively for their future independence.

This recognises that some young people will have become irremediably alienated from school; several pupils at this unit had previously passed through one of the local school-based units but had been unable to accept even that form of schooling. They do not necessarily, however, lack the incentive to learn; it has been found that most have very clear ideas about the skills they wish to develop and the unit staff respond to this by drawing up individual educational programmes.

The fourth 'unit' is also for pupils in their final year of secondary schooling and who are described as unwilling and experiencing or causing considerable difficulties. Here, however, steps have been taken to avoid any negative connotations which might attach to the creation of a special unit; the provision in this case is in the form of a special course at a College of Further Education. It is known as an Extended Vocational Link Course (EVLC) and provides up to twelve places for pupils at secondary schools in a wide area of the county.

The initiative for this came from the college which had previously run day release link courses and had also accepted a number of less able students. The proposal involved the appointment of two remedial education specialists to organise programmes of work for the referred pupils which related to their individual interests and had a vocational bias. It was explicitly stated that there was no intention to provide 'therapy' or 'special education'; the general aims included encouraging the pupils to work with others, attempting 'to rekindle the curiosity and confidence that they appear to have lost' and helping them to find employment.

This scheme, which started in 1978, gives an opportunity for its pupils to integrate with students on existing vocational courses in the college whilst providing separate facilities in which additional remedial help, pastoral care and further curriculum work can be given by the special course tutors. Transfer to the EVLC after the end of the fourth year is by consent of both parent and pupil and after acceptance of the referral by an admissions panel. This consists of a senior inspector from the local authority, the area education officer, a head teacher and a head of department in the College of Further Education. The schools psychology service and the social services department may make referrals but in this case are not involved in selecting candidates.

Pupils' perceptions

The material presented in this section is intended to give an impression of the experience of special units and troubled secondary schooling from the point of view of pupils in these situations. It is based on data collected from a total of thirty-two pupils (nineteen boys and thirteen girls) attending the four units described above. In three of the units, the material was derived from group interviews which were conducted in a fairly informal way, though an interview schedule was drawn up to provide a structure for the discussions. This identified the main areas of focus and included a series of probe questions to be used as necessary. Originally it was intended to tape-record these interviews to provide as full a record as possible but in two cases it was obvious that the recorder was seriously inhibiting the discussion, so it was not used. On these two occasions, brief notes were made during the discussion and fuller accounts written up from memory immediately afterwards.

With students on the EVLC a different method of data collecting was used. On an initial visit to this unit, one group interview was conducted and the impression was gained that these young people would be well disposed to the idea of writing their observations. It was decided in this case to collect written data; a number of questions, based on the interview schedule, were specified and the students wrote down their answers. These varied in length and detail and they revealed wide variations in ability; in the case of one girl with limited skill in writing, her answers were dictated to the teacher and typed.

It was clear at the time that the group interview was an appropriate way of stimulating pupils in the other three units to express their ideas and feelings. An impression was given that written work of any kind was one of the less popular activities. It is interesting, therefore, to consider why pupils in the fourth group, who were not differentiated from the others in terms of their ability or previous school experience (in general terms), should seem more willing to indulge in writing. One explanation might be that while conventional units put stress on non-classroom-like

activities and on group meetings designed to encourage verbal-
isation, the EVLC enables its clients to identify not with those
who have failed in the education system and been rejected by it
but with FE students who have achieved some relative success.
Thus it is possible that opportunities to engage in student-like
activities would be more readily grasped by this group. In any
event, they appeared to enjoy the exercise and produced some
frank and informative data.

It should be stressed here that this small-scale study has limited
aims. It is not intended in itself to compensate for the lack of a
pupil's perspective on the unit phenomenon which has been
missing from the existing literature. As it concentrates on a
narrow range of questions it cannot claim to describe the social
reality of special units from their point of view. This would be a
valuable contribution for sociology to make to our understanding of special units but it would require a somewhat more elaborate methodology to meet the problem of identifying authentic
meanings, incorporating methods which ideally would include
observations of actual behaviour in face-to-face situations
encountered in the units. In this more limited enterprise, the
object is simply to represent the views of a number of unit pupils
on their recent experience, to indicate in a limited way the meanings they attach to being a unit pupil and to having been a
problem pupil in their secondary schools. This could perhaps be
likened to a preliminary stage in a more extensive investigation
of pupils' definitions but for the present will be simply used
to identify certain themes and draw together some of the key
issues.

1 Perceptions of the units

The pupils were first of all asked to indicate what it was like to be
in a unit; most of the responses were in terms of what they liked
best about it and many made actual or implied comparisons with
school. The most common type of observation related to the way
they perceived their treatment in the unit, reflecting in particular
a feeling of greater freedom and an absence of oppressive restric-
tion:

'Being on the EVLC is different from school because you
have more freedom and you're treated older.'

'The differences are you are treated as adults and we discuss
our prospects for the future in more detail.'

'... you have a sense of responsibility, you are trusted.'

'I'll do better here because you can smoke and [there's] no uniform.'

'... no uniform, you can wear what you like.'

'You don't get bossed about by teachers.'

The unit teacher is clearly regarded as performing a different role from that of teachers in ordinary schools, the abiding impression of whom, for many of these young people, is of authoritarian, punitive figures. The unit teachers, on the other hand, are seen in a very different light, less judgemental and more caring:

'The teachers don't look down on you everywhere you go, you don't feel like a criminal.'

'The difference in being here ... is if you get in trouble the teacher doesn't give you the cane, they talk to you and treat you like grown-ups and not like babies, like they do at school. If I got in trouble with the police I would phone up any one of the teachers here and they will come down and put a good word in for me.'

'The teachers are kind and they treat you better where they didn't at school.'

'Also at this college the teachers are more fair with you like if you got done by the screws at school you were finished but here you are given a fair chance and are expected to repay the college by behaving.'

Initial questioning in the group interviews often elicited jocular responses (there was a good deal of humour expressed generally in the groups). 'We have a good laugh here' was a frequent remark and appears to represent an important feature of units for many of the pupils. As Woods (1976) has argued, 'having a laugh' has a number of functions for school pupils and in his perceptive paper based on acutely observed data from a rural secondary school, he describes its various forms and purposes, together with the rules which control it. In the units, 'having a laugh' seems to be in Woods' terms, 'mucking about' behaviour rather than subversive laughter aimed at undermining the teacher's authority. In this case, 'mucking about' is not so much an antidote to boredom but rather a legitimate activity jointly carried out by pupils and teachers.

'It's easier to get on with adults at this school because they are friendlier and easier to talk to and they'll have a good laugh with you.'

'When we're in "Gold" we have a good laugh ... yeah ... We go out a lot and that's OK ... Now I've been in "Gold" I say it's a good laugh and we have some good lessons ... Outings is good.'

Outings and trips were often mentioned among the advantages of being in a unit and the opinion almost universally expressed that the unit was preferable to school because there was more variety in the activities provided. Comments referring in general terms to the curriculum and organisation show that the units' flexibility was greatly appreciated:

'You get a choice about what you'd like to do and most of the things you ask for you can do.'

'You're not pressured here, not *made* to do things you don't want to do.'

'You can spend more time on one thing instead of an hour on each thing like at [school].'

'I'll think I'll do better here because there's more to do. Most of the lessons you get here you wouldn't get at school unless you came down to tech' for a day.'

When asked whether they thought they were being helped by the unit, most pupils were able to reply that they were. Typical responses were:

'I've actually done work since I've been here. I never did any at [school], I was never there.'

'I don't lose my temper so much now. I can make friends easier.'

'I feel more relaxed since I came here. I don't have the urge to disappear all the time.'

Several pupils indicated that they saw referral to the unit as a last chance to salvage something from their educational careers and in some responses there was perhaps a recognition that they needed to escape from negative stereotyping:

'I will do better here because I will make a fresh start.'

'While I'm here I've got to improve my behaviour and work hard to get good results ... I've got to.'

'I don't stay off like I did at [school] because I want to make a go of my schooling and have some qualifications when I do leave.'

'I think I'll be all right here because there are people who I've never met before and they don't know that I've got kicked out of school and they will treat me like a normal student.'

2 Perceptions of school

It is of course to be expected that pupils who had been persistent truants or who had repeatedly been in trouble at school would look back on their school careers with some distaste. And in the sample from the four units there was accordingly a universal negative response to enquiries about what school had been like. Most of them were expressed as a generalised reaction, for example: '... boring – just boring', 'I just couldn't bear to go, it was like a prison camp to me', though specific aspects of school life were mentioned in some cases. The majority of these referred to the actions or the attitudes of teachers and it would appear that for most of these pupils 'school' meant 'the teachers'. A few references were made to aspects of the curriculum, though seldom in a direct way, and occasionally other pupils were mentioned but by and large the responses expressed irritation about the teachers with whom they had formerly had dealings:

'... the teachers pick on you.'

'Teachers don't bother they are more concerned about the brainy ones.'

'... school was too strict, the teachers only like to teach the higher class.'

'Teachers are too old-fashioned, they need more young teachers who know more about young people.'

'The only time they bothered was when they knew they could get me into trouble.'

'I didn't like school because the teachers thought they was hard, they were not, they just made you laugh and when you played up they just couldn't cope.'

Questions about particular difficulties experienced at school elicited more abundant responses than any other question. These reveal a picture of classic disaffection, of troubled children whose needs the schools have been unable to meet and whose deviant behaviour has exacerbated the problem increasing the antipathy between school and pupil until each has rejected the other. Phrases like 'I don't like lessons', 'I couldn't get on' and 'They didn't want me' do not of course explain the root causes of the dissonance but they can be taken as descriptions of the problem in as far as it is comprehensible to the pupils concerned. Such expressions reveal how *they* perceive the problem and represent the meanings *they* attach to their experience of failure to adapt to the demands of school. These are some typical responses:

'I didn't like it so I never went a lot. When I did go I was nearly always late and I used to get into trouble a lot.'

'My problem at school was I didn't like most of my lessons and I didn't get on with the teachers at all and all I did was skive school a lot.'

'I just couldn't get on at [school] so I gave up trying. When I gave up working, the teachers gave up teaching so I just didn't think it was worth going so I never went. I used to go in, get my mark and then walk out and go home.'

'They didn't want me at school because I was never there and I was cheeky.'

'My problems were that I hated most of the teachers and I hated sitting in lesson all day getting bored stiff and usually I had other things on my mind and I used to think that the teachers were picking on me so I used to be cheeky and bitchy to them.'

Many of the respondents mentioned specific incidents which they regarded either as typifying their difficulties or as marking a significant moment in their history of trouble at school. Often these were described in tones which communicated a sense of resignation but in many cases resentment was the dominant mood.

'My problem really was that I didn't get on with one teacher and once he pushed me too far and I lost my temper and threw a desk at him and threatened him with a hammer.'

'Once I was told to hold the door open by a teacher to let all the other people get out. When they had all gone I let the door slam and the teacher came back and kicked me. I told the headmistress and she said I must have done something else to have deserved it. I told my mum and she rang up and she got an apology but I didn't.'

A third example is a lengthy account written by one of the students on the EVLC. It is quoted here at length since it describes a sequence of events paralleled in several other instances. It would appear to be, for the pupil concerned, an encapsulation of his developing career as a deviant pupil.

'I had no trouble in the 1st, 2nd and 3rd year ... it all started one day when I got fed up with a lesson and the teacher told me to do something and I told her to get stuffed and she told the head, he sent me for the cane. Then I started skiving lessons and days and weeks at a time and I had so much time off they started looking into it ... they gave me a warning ... I started having days and weeks off being as every day I went there, the teacher would have a go at me and I would go and tell the head and [he] would not take any notice of me and say get back to your lesson ... I remember one occasion I was at home and the school board officer [EWO] came round to my house and he said I would have to go to school and if I got into trouble he would help me. And when I went back to school I got in trouble the first day and I went to see him and he was not there. The next time I went to school with some jeans on and the teacher told me to go and get some more trousers on which were black. [Mine had] been ripped and thrown away and my mum was going to get me some new ones at the weekend so I went to the man and told him and he said that I should do what I was told. So I went home, got in and I found some big baggy trousers so I put them on and went back to school and when I got there this boy turned to laugh at me and I beat him up and the head master give me the cane ... At the end of the fourth year a teacher sent for me and said he was going to give me the cane and I got in first and give it him and ran out. I never went back again.'

Although this is one of the more extreme cases, it is typical of a sizable proportion of the unit children interviewed: those whose home and family circumstances had created considerable strain for them and led to their being seriously disadvantaged in the context of school. The recollections of the boy quoted above would seem to suggest that his school was unable to adapt itself to deal with this small minority of pupils with severe problems and his story suggests, furthermore, that his behaviour difficulties were amplified by policies of the school which demanded the harsh use of punitive sanctions and the rigid enforcement of rules with some of which it was impossible for him to comply.

The interviewees were questioned about the help they were given at school when their problems arose and several recalled particular teachers who had obviously shown sympathy and made efforts to be fair and supportive. One pupil remembered a deputy head who would always 'listen to both sides and find out who was really to blame'. But this man, it seemed to the pupil describing the events, was always overruled by the headmistress who 'just wouldn't listen, she just caned you'. So although there were a few positive, if lukewarm, references to previous relationships with teachers, the overwhelming impression is that this was a group of young people whose experience had given them a strong antipathy to teachers as a breed and who had become resigned to the inevitability of being constantly in conflict with them.

Discussion

It is difficult to escape the impression from the various surveys of unit provision (Topping and Quelch 1976; DES 1978b; ACE 1980; Topping 1983) that this type of resource became a panic response during a period of widespread alarm over an apparent increase in the incidence of disruptive and violent behaviour among school pupils. It was a patently superficial response: the question posed and answered was 'How can we contain the difficult pupils?' More profound and more important questions appear to have been ignored by the majority of school heads and educational administrators – questions such as 'Why does the problem seem to be getting more acute?', 'Why do some pupils have difficulty in conforming to the behavioural expectations of the school?' and 'Can schools change in order to make such behaviour less likely to occur?'

A clear indication is given in the information obtained from unit pupils for this study (see also Galwey 1979) that the specific difficulties they have encountered are related to things over which teachers *do* have control, such as the curriculum, organisation and teacher–pupil relationships. It is not adequate, therefore, to point only to external factors at neighbourhood or societal level and conclude that schools are not themselves concerned in the generation of their pupils' problematic and disturbing behaviour. There is no question that the majority of disruptive pupils unfortunately suffer from disadvantages in their domestic circumstances and these sometimes produce constant strain which is very difficult for others to perceive or appreciate. These pupils are thus extremely vulnerable to additional strains and where these occur, disturbed behaviour is likely to result. It should be recognised that certain taken-for-granted requirements of school curricula and organisation create strain for all pupils; most of it is tolerable for all pupils, some of it is intolerable for a few. The majority of school pupils can accept that some aspects of the curriculum will be boring and will seem to be irrelevant, and that certain school regulations are petty and demeaning. The strain created by these things, however, is easily absorbed by the majority. For the child undergoing a high degree of stressful experience elsewhere, these minor strains become major problems. The vulnerable child's repertoire of skills for dealing with problems may, furthermore, be extremely limited and the solution adopted may sometimes be inappropriate. If teachers were able to reduce some of these secondary strains, acts of disruption and rebellion would be less likely to happen.

The observations made by unit pupils repeatedly brought relationships with particular teachers into the forefront of their perceptions of schooling. One significant 'type' projected by these comments is an intolerant and hypercritical person who is content when dealing with able, conforming and well-motivated children but who has little concern for the less able and little desire or ability to appreciate the personal problems of pupils – a good example, in fact, of the 'deviance provocative' teacher (see Jordan 1974, cited in Hargreaves 1975).

The pupils' recollections of relationships with such teachers suggest the operation of a process which would tend to exacerbate problems. This can be comprehended in sociological terms as the process in which a reaction to what is formally or informally defined by teachers as deviation, produces further or secondary deviation. The pupil with problems inexorably becomes the problem pupil. It is therefore important to raise the question of whether the extreme and dramatic response of setting up a special unit and thereby creating a characteristic status and set of non-normal or disrupted educational experiences for a particular group of pupils, might not have the effect of amplifying deviance within a school or school district.

This is a question which unfortunately defies easy solution by empirical investigation and certainly the existing evidence has little light to shed on the issue. In one sense, of course, the adoption of the unit strategy automatically leads to an increase in the number of pupils whose deviance is considered serious enough to require separate treatment: there is a self-fulfilling effect in the policy. But it is less easy to determine influences on the self-concepts of those pupils involved and on their subsequent careers: to measure any qualitative effects of the policy as opposed to quantitative ones. Some of the evidence would suggest that units can exert a positive influence on self-perceptions: by removing the pupil from the scene of failure and conflict they can give opportunities for success and more satisfactory relationships with teachers and fellow pupils. Several writers have also mentioned the fact that for school leavers seeking employment, units can bring tangible benefits, something which might be assumed to have a positive effect on self-esteem.

However, it would be a mistake to separate units from the events and the institutional processes through which the pupils have passed before being admitted. The unit is merely one phase in a deviant career. Hence, as will have been apparent throughout this concluding discussion, there is a crucial question underlying the specific issue of special units, a question about the responses in general which the school makes to deviant pupil behaviour. The point about possible deviance-amplifying effects of units thus becomes subordinate to this general question which draws attention to the internal operation of schools, in particular the differentiating mechanisms and social processes which have a powerful effect on pupil outcomes.

The final proposition offered is this: the sudden proliferation of special units in the 1970s bears an important message, not about a decline in behavioural standards among the young but about changes taking place in schools. The efforts involved in setting up these new resources, the public discussion of their purposes and methods and the evaluation of their success, all serve to divert attention away from causes of educational breakdown which exist within schools themselves. Many schools, it seems, are unable to deal effectively with the vulnerable and difficult child, or are unwilling to try. Some schools obviously can rise successfully to these challenges (see DES 1978c), providing regimes which encourage constructive and supportive relationships and avoiding policies which might exacerbate problems, but many clearly cannot.

Amongst the groups of pupils who are currently collected together in special units is a small proportion who undoubtedly require an alternative to large classes and complicated timetables in what seems to them disturbingly complex organisations, perhaps on a permanent basis if their education is to be successfully completed. But the rest, the large majority, could have survived in conventional school situations if their problems had been sensitively recognised and the schools had been able to respond flexibly to their needs. The conflict and misdemeanours which marked them out as pupils requiring to be segregated from their peers and their regular teachers could in many cases have been avoided. There is an urgent need for schools to develop a deeper understanding of pupils' difficulties and to utilise a wider range of techniques and arrangements for dealing with them. Disruption in schools is a problem which could be diminished dramatically if the principle of prevention rather than cure were to guide the schools' responses to it.

7
The creation of the disruptive pupil

David Coulby

This chapter is principally concerned with those aspects of school life likely to encourage disruptive behaviour among pupils. It will also consider the wider framework of educational ideas and processes which increase the likelihood that a fraction of the school population may be stigmatised as disruptive. In locating the generation of disruptive behaviour firmly within the context of the school, the intention is not so much to counter the explanations which would use home background to account for it but rather to sidestep them. These explanations have been widely voiced in the past (e.g. Laslett 1977) but much recent writing has tended to criticise them (Grunsell 1980b; Tomlinson 1981 and 1982; Barton and Tomlinson 1981; Thomas and Swann 1982; Booth 1982a). There may well be tangible elements within a child's home circumstances – physical mistreatment or lack of adequate nourishment – which generate a predisposition towards anti-authority or troublesome behaviour in school. But these predispositions are either fulfilled or frustrated within the social contexts of the school and the classroom. Research has shown that schools vary in their tendencies to encourage such and similar predispositions (Power *et al.* 1967; Power *et al.* 1972; Rutter *et al.* 1979) and professional experience suggests that within the same school some teachers are more likely than others to elicit disruptive behaviour. To concentrate on the school context, however, need not be to revel in another opportunity to criticise those shortcomings of heads and teachers apparently so obvious from the academic sidelines. Rather in attempting to examine the processes whereby schools generate disruptive behaviour, it may be possible to suggest areas of change or alternative procedures likely to minimise such behaviour. Many such successful procedures are already part of what might be regarded as good school practice, so the discussion will focus on practice and indeed my own experience of working with so-called disruptive children in an inner city area as well as on academic sources.

At the outset one may wonder if the creation of the disruptive pupil is not largely a matter of attaching a specific label or creating an institutional category. Special units for disruptive pupils have mushroomed during the past decade (DES 1978b; Booth 1982b) despite the apparently parallel provisions inside many local education authorities of special schools for the maladjusted, tutorial classes and so on. Whether this growth of provision was necessitated by a breakdown of discipline in schools (Thornbury 1978) is debatable. Their creation may have been a concession on the part of authorities attempting to abolish corporal punishment or to allay the fears of teachers with regard to the onset of comprehensive education. Once the units were established by some authorities pressure could be placed on others to follow suit. In many ways the units are an ideal administrative solution. Since they do not have the status of schools there is no need to pay head teacher salaries or to take undue notice of the person responsible, who is only a teacher-in-charge. Outside the statutory special education system there is no need to seek the possibly heterodoxical opinions of educational psychologists or even parents. Largely controlled by head teachers the units provide them with a way of responding directly to the demand of hard pressed teachers. On grounds such as these the very legality of the units was questioned by the Scarman Report (Home Office 1981), and criticism elsewhere has been frequent (for example, Francis 1980a): the point here is that once the provision had been created a category of pupils was accepted as a feature of mainstream schools. It was unlikely that the units would be left empty; pupils could as easily be found to fill the category as teachers, psychologists and theorists to legitimate its existence. The growth of the so-called hyperactive syndrome in the USA (Schrag and Divoky 1981) is a parallel phenomenon. The giving of institutional validity to the category of disruptive pupils may be regarded as a major contribution to their creation: it remained only to isolate individuals and slot them into the existing label and provision. Whether their removal results in an actual decrease in classroom disruption is a different matter, though if a few children disappear ominously to the 'sin bin' this may well serve *pour encourager les autres*.

It is perhaps not too perverse then to ask whether or not there is such a phenomenon as the disruptive pupil apart from the institutional categorisation. Are the same children disruptive in all lessons, at all times of the day and week, with all teachers? Are they disruptive at home and at the youth club as well as at school? Surely much more common is the occurrence of selective disruption at various times, places and tasks. Nor is disruption necessarily a piece of irrational adolescent exuberance. Rosser and Harré (1976) have shown that it may have valid reasons and rules for the protagonists. It is then perhaps preferable to think of children whose behaviour is in some contexts disruptive to the teacher's perception of positive academic progress. Crucially, disruptive is a word more appropriately applied to behaviour than to people. In this way any shadow of the medical model with its tendency to confuse the handicap with the person (Potts 1982a) may be avoided. It might then be possible to ask what these behaviours are which are construed to be disruptive and who has the power to define them as such. The use of behaviour-specific descriptions (Lane 1978a and 1978b; Leach and Raybould 1977) would be helpful here, but it is also necessary to understand how even such accurately assessed behaviours fall within a definition of disruptive. If the categorisation of pupils as disruptive is seen to be invalid then it may further be recognised that the classification of behaviours as disruptive within a specific context implies a moral or 'professional' judgement on the part of one or more of the participants. It is usually the teachers who possess the power to have their definitions institutionally accepted. Such definitions will vary from school to school and from teacher to teacher: the head of maths, for instance, may well perceive disruption in what the young drama teacher understands to be a creative, imaginative and cathartic group experience. More obviously the definitions may vary between the teacher, the pupil or pupils concerned and the rest of the class: Willis's lads do not talk about classroom disruption but about 'having a laff' (Willis 1977). A position of such relativism need not prevent one from understanding the discomfort and waste of many disrupted lessons. Nevertheless, the creation of the disruptive pupil has in part been achieved through the use of this sloppy term itself and in its reification into an institutional category.

The elements of schooling in primary and secondary schools likely to facilitate disruption may be studied under four broad headings: curriculum, pedagogy, organisation and peer group. In

practice there is much interrelation and overlap betv
The wider legitimisations of the disruptive pupil categ
operate on the school context include the theory and p
educational psychology, the practice of special educa
professionalisation of disruptive units and the status of academic
achievement.

Curriculum

Midwinter's strictures on the curriculum remain valid, as do his
recommendations that it should be useful, first-hand, develop-
mental, interesting and understandable (Midwinter 1977).
Nevertheless it is easier to sneer at unimaginative failure than to
suggest what a group of 14-year-olds will find relevant etc. on a
windy Wednesday afternoon – apart from each other. But some
criticisms must be mentioned before suggesting more positive
alternatives. Unfortunately the curriculum in the UK still contains large elements of covert and overt racism: the former may
be exemplified in the use of the reading scheme *Pirates* (a favourite
for 'remedial' children who stand a higher chance of being black
or 'disruptive' or both); the latter is seen in many history courses
which accept uncritically the nineteenth-century imperial dream,
or in English courses where culture is taken to be the exclusive
product of one continent. Where such a curriculum exists some
disaffection among black pupils may not be too surprising; it
could indeed be seen as a rational response of resistance.

The gender stereotypes of the *Ladybird* scheme or the wood-
work and computer studies versus home economics and office
practice time-table may cause parallel resentments among girls.
But at the same time this curriculum induces an ideological
control whereby the acting out of such feelings would be considered unfeminine. This argument may indeed be generalised to
all working-class pupils. If the knowledge and curriculum of the
school are seen to be the exclusive product and prerogative of the
elite, children are likely to perceive them as separate from and
potentially alien to their own experience. If the culture of the
child is belittled or ignored in the school whilst an alternative is
handed down (be it nature study, conservation or Shakespeare)
then again resentment against the teacher's view of what is
worthwhile may be far from irrational. At first sight disruptive
behaviour may seem to have little connection with school knowledge: it is hard to see spitting on younger children or destroying

another pupil's property as any kind of premeditated response to being subjected to middle-class knowledge. Nevertheless, the actual content of school knowledge may well play its part in the long process of disillusionment with education. To ignore such disillusionment and to seek the cause of disruptive behaviour in the psychopathology of individual pupils is to do a disservice to the education of all children.

Practical suggestions for more positive curricula abound (e.g. Wasp 1980). It may be possible to isolate those strands helpful to a curriculum which would not encourage classroom disruption: the development of skills, economically marketable knowledge, localism. Teaching which is designed to equip pupils with definite skills is perhaps the least likely to be subjected to disruption. This is most obvious in the fascination pupils have in learning to master equipment such as VDUs, typewriters, bunsen burners, spanners etc. The motivation towards learning foreign languages, however, may also be dramatically increased when it is a matter of chatting up the locals rather than taking a test. This is one of the main principles behind the pragmatic curriculum developed by Dewey and transferred to some UK primary schools as learning by doing. Whilst by no means an infallible curricular criterion it may occasionally be worth teachers asking themselves what exactly they are teaching, if they are not teaching skills.

Teachers rarely see it as essential that the knowledge they transmit should have some value on the job market. Parents, children and those who speak for the disadvantaged (Field 1977) have a rather different view. There is some overlap here with the issue of skills, but more central is the question of the relationship between the school and the workplace. In the Soviet education system, the polytechnical curriculum is being developed (Castles and Wustenberg 1979). This is not so much a subject as a method by which all subjects are to be learnt. Children learn about the workplace, they visit factories, farms and offices and experience working in them; the relevance of their school learning to the practices and ideology of the workplace is constantly stressed. The separation between school and work in the UK may be one of the elements in the creation of adolescence as a problematic and alienated interim (Erikson 1968). Work experience and bridging courses are ways in which this separation is currently being eroded, but if a more polytechnical approach to the whole curriculum were to be adopted this might increase many pupils' perceptions of the validity and usefulness of schooling. Of course this would be undermined if polytechnical education were seen to be an inferior option for the potentially disaffected while their more placid peers continue to study for eight O levels. The reorganisation of the education of 16–19-year-olds may well provide opportunities for innovation. Nevertheless, the separation between school and work becomes all the more evident in times of high unemployment: if even well qualified pupils are not getting jobs what, many ask, is the point of bothering with schoolwork at all? Education for unemployment will be seen to have relevance only if it avoids the trap of teaching expensive middle class hobbies and focuses instead on how teenagers can stay organised, fit, in touch with each other, aware of possibilities and in contact with those fortunate enough to be in work.

Localism as an element in the school curriculum may be criticised on the grounds that the school should not teach things the children probably already know more about than the teachers; that the pupils' experiences and imaginations must be stretched beyond their own backgrounds. It has, however, been demonstrated (Searle 1973) that a local element in the curriculum need not be restrictive and that it can be successful in urban schools not unfamiliar with disruption. The wider issue of who does and who should control the school curriculum is one currently vexing both politicians and educationists (Lawton 1980; Apple 1979). The suggestion here is that any kind of knowledge determined outside the classroom context and presented to pupils as beyond the subject of their discussion or even experience is likely to be received as alienating. The nature and content of school knowledge could be opened to a dialogue in which the backgrounds and experiences of different groups of children could be used as the basis for curriculum planning as much as or more than the elitist culture and knowledge often espoused by the teachers. Curriculum change in the direction of greater dialogue and of generating pragmatic and polytechnical approaches may well benefit the education of most pupils: there is also the possibility that in this way school knowledge may not play a part in the creation of the disruptive pupil.

Pedagogy

The concern here is not so much with that heraldic creature the good teacher, but rather with those aspects of pedagogy which contribute to the creation of classroom disruption and more positively what types of teacher behaviour can serve to minimise such incidents. When a teacher arrives late, hands back homework unmarked after three weeks and initiates lessons which seem to lack either plans or direction, that teacher's own credibility will be impaired and respect lost or never attained, and the pupils' confidence in the general enterprise of schooling will be undermined. At first this is likely to lead to behaviour which is not compatible with the aims of the teacher – private conversations, horseplay, comic reading, card games – but in addition cynical and anti-authority attitudes and behaviours will be encouraged which may subsequently spread to other lessons or to corridors, staircases and the playground. If the teacher concerned challenges the incompatible behaviours and adopts a threatening or punitive stance, pupil resentment is quite likely to lead to non-compliance, confrontation and abuse. Once again it is possible to see classroom disruption as a rational and potentially valid response. The example here is flagrant but similar analyses could be made of teacher behaviours such as remaining sitting at the desk, the use of punitive sarcasm, overlooking bullying, demanding impossible standards, personal rudeness and physical punishment.

What then are the practices and styles which teachers can adopt which are likely to minimise incidents of classroom disruption? In an article in *The Times Educational Supplement* (10 October 1982) Jude Collins argues against academic reluctance to provide 'tips for teachers': 'My feeling is that helpful hints should be passed on unashamedly and frequently.' Thus encouraged, it is possible to make some far from comprehensive positive suggestions which might be preferable to a list of facile criticisms of bad practice. The Collins article is followed on the next page by a brief article of advice by McManus which focuses specifically on difficult classes. His trenchancy provides an excellent approach: 'One of the key factors in keeping control in the classroom is keeping them busy. Provide plenty of work and vary the activities and tasks.' Some consideration for the appropriateness of the curricular material is also essential, as mentioned above. A varied sequence of tasks is more likely to retain interest and momentum as well as offering opportunities for different individual skills, but this needs organisation and smooth, enthusiastic management. Rules and expectations should be clear and exact. They should be repeated often and applied consistently. It is best not to have unnecessary rules: the fewer the better. What rules there are need to be understood and, whenever possible, agreed by the pupils. This tends to involve repetition with younger children and moral discussion in secondary classes: in both cases this is likely to be effective and educationally valid. Exceptions can be made, and, as McManus points out, other children will usually accept this if the reasons are made clear. Flexibility within a framework of consistency (perhaps the central paradox of pedagogical judgement) is essential with regard to both the curriculum and standards of behaviour. The alternative can be a sequence of unnecessary confrontations caused by the teacher thinking that every child must perform and behave up to some abstractly determined standard.

One of the ways, often neglected, in which a teacher can impart a positive influence on lessons is by control of the classroom environment. Elements in the teacher's control are the seating of the pupils and himself or herself (who sits next to whom, what size of groups, how composed and arranged), displays on walls, tables and blackboard, positioning of equipment, and general tidiness and appearance. All these can make a considerable difference to a lesson and need to be planned and adjusted according to varying needs. Sometimes a sleepy, grumpy class on a wet afternoon can be brought back to concentration by the simple expedient of opening the windows. This awareness of the classroom environment may also include the physical organisation of lessons. Queues at the teacher's desk, for instance, often indicate that many children are wasting time waiting instead of working; they also block the teacher's vision and attention and make it easy for the rest of the class to stray from their tasks. The positioning of the teacher and the teacher's desk are important as is the ability of the teacher to move smoothly about the room. If the teacher is mobile in the classroom, paying attention to children's work, initiating and contributing to discussion and praising good work as well as helping with problems, the class is likely to be studying positively. The lesson topics can then be dealt with before boredom or frustration is compounded into disruption.

As a general strategy it is better for the teacher to be approaching than retreating, better to be setting and assessing work than complaining about misbehaviour, better to be in among the desks than sitting behind his or her own, better to be aware of everything happening in the classroom rather than hoping trouble will go away. Eye contact can be useful: sometimes the ability to meet a pupil's eye obviates the necessity for a reprimand. Even if this does not work the teacher is in a much stronger position if the approach to any disruption is early, swift and with eyes on the participants. There is a danger in concentrating too much on one or two disruptive acts to the neglect of the progress of the class as a whole. Again McManus' advice is to the point: 'Don't neglect the group when dealing with one problem child. Keep your eyes roving and make remarks to show you're not missing anything.' Such remarks should be positive and encouraging rather than an indication of any kind of total prohibitive surveillance.

It is more effective to reward than to punish and the most readily available reward is praise from the teacher. This is best when detailed and directed to academic performance, not just the blanket 'good' but pointing out precisely what has been success-fully achieved. The swifter the praise or any reward follows the performance the more effective it is likely to be. More tangible rewards may be used, particularly preferred tasks or activities. Rather than a straight trade off or bribe the teacher may prefer to reward a small group for one or two pupils' successful attain-ment, thereby gaining the support and encouragement of the group for the specified task. When tangible rewards are used it may be necessary to offer some explanation to the rest of the class, though children are often subtly aware of the different personalities within their groups and the commensurately varied demands these make on the teacher. Where such awareness seems to be lacking or there is fear of singling out one child too much even for reward, it is possible to make a treat for the entire class contingent on successful performance by one child. Although peer group pressure may assist the teacher in this case, it is rather a strong force and may work against the long-term interests of the child; it could lead to physical pressure being exerted or to the creation of a class baby. Such elaborate tech-niques are best used with caution and only after the normal procedures of praise and encouragement have been seen to fail. Inappropriate classroom behaviour may be reinforced by the teacher attention it elicits, even if this is negative or punitive. Yet the policy of ignoring such behaviour is rarely possible and in a secondary school it could prove disastrous. It may, however, be possible to minimise the attention received as a result of such behaviour. Quiet remarks to individual pupils are more likely to improve behaviour than shouted, negative and public comments. It is probably best for the teacher always to be seen to be aware of what is happening in the lesson and to disapprove of what is not appropriate to its progress. Physical punishment provides pupils with an undesirable example of violent authority and is ineffective as well as being inhumane. Other punishments are likely to be effective only if the pupil understands precisely why they have been incurred and if the teacher ensures that they are appropriately performed.

McManus' final advice concerns confrontations. If the appropriate curriculum and teaching methods are used, one would hope that these could be avoided. Confrontations tend to increase the likelihood of an unsettled atmosphere in the next lesson for both the teacher and pupils. They are a sign that inappropriate behaviour has become more important than the academic progress of the lesson. Whenever they can be avoided without undue loss of control this is probably the best course. However, once a confrontation has occurred, McManus offers three useful rules to the teacher: 'At the end of any confrontation you should have done three things: separated the act from the actor; clearly stated the re-opening terms; defined the event for the benefit of the audience, if one is present.' This section has concentrated on techniques for avoiding confrontations and disruptive behaviour in general: by implication the type of pedagogy likely to encourage the creation of the disruptive pupil is not hard to descry.

School organisation

As in the last section it is possible either to point to types of school organisation likely to generate disruptive behaviour or to those which keep it to a minimum. The discussion, here while moving away from 'tips for teachers', does retain direct relevance for practice. Considerations of curriculum and pedagogy need to be made from a wider perspective in terms of the whole school, but similar principles are likely to apply. School rules, for instance, like classroom rules, should be kept to a minimum, be easily understood, have an open rationale which pupils can share and be subjected to frequent repetition and discussion. If discussion with pupils leads to the rules being modified, so much the better. Many school rules such as those concerned with dress, appearance and superficial conduct such as chewing gum, seem designed to provide opportunities for defiance and confrontation. One could argue that if children are consistently getting into trouble for having their top buttons undone they will not risk any more serious misbehaviour. But to have teachers and pupils literally at each other's throats over such a trivial issue would not seem to encourage a positive atmosphere directed towards educational work. Where such rules are removed it is possible that pupils will find other causes for defiance, but at least teachers might be able to defend these causes with more conviction and make an appeal to a wider part of the school constituency. Rules concerning violence, swearing, racism and smoking are likely to lead to quite fruitful discussions in which the teacher's authority will have the support of many pupils as well as that of the wider community.

That teachers provide adult models for pupils is more obvious at primary than secondary school. Older children are influenced by the behaviour of their teachers but they are likely to be more discerning in their admirations and to resent hypocrisy. This is hardly too strong a word for the dual standards of dress, attendance, behaviour (such as smoking) and even language which some teachers seek to operate. The difficulty tends to occur where some of the teachers do not endorse the rules of the school, where the young punk teacher with vivid, dyed hair and a ring through his ear has to compel the pupils in his tutor group to wear school ties. Such confrontations may be avoided by judicious change in the school rules, but there will nevertheless be variations in commitment among members of staff to specific rules and differences in the enthusiasm with which they are enforced. While one would not advocate the cloning of teachers, the greater the consistency among the staff, the greater the likelihood that pupils will take rules seriously, resulting in fewer confrontations over minor acts of defiance. The school organisation may perhaps encourage such consistency by providing opportunities for discussion and consultation.

Perhaps the major element in school organisations which leads to the creation of disruptive pupils is streaming (Hargreaves 1967; Corrigan 1979). In secondary schools some older children may come to see themselves as simply batting out time until they leave with little possibility of educational or examination success. They may then turn their attention to other interests which are either outside the classroom or directed against teachers and lessons. The examination system in the UK, which effectively makes failures of most pupils by the age of sixteen, is partly responsible for such apathy and rebellion. However, schools have some choice over which subjects and examinations are taken and how the teaching groups are organised. Mode 3 CSEs in mixed-ability groups may offer an intense and stretching curriculum even if, at present, not every pupil can obtain a good pass. The creation of educational ghettoes is not the prerogative of rigid streaming, it may come about by offering an alternative, and blatantly inferior, curriculum to those whom teachers consider to be less able. There is a considerable overlap between those pupils considered least able and those perceived as troublesome in lessons (Tomlinson 1981). ILEA research (see Coard 1977) has shown that referral to a school for maladjusted pupils has in the vast majority of cases been preceded by learning failure. Whether backwardness and difficult behaviour necessarily go inherently together may be doubted. It is perhaps more plausible to see lack of academic success leading to frustration and attempts to acquire esteem in other ways. Similarly, referral to remedial classes or ESN(M) schools as well as placements in less academic forms or subject areas may be due to a child's being considered difficult and likely to inhibit the 'progress' of the 'bright' groups, rather than to any lack of ability. Much disruptive behaviour in non-academic forms of secondary schools may then be seen as the creation of the organisation of the school which groups stigmatised children together and subjects them to an inferior curriculum, often with the worst equipment and with either the least effective teachers or the staff bullies.

Even remedial and special classes or groups (under whatever reformative or alternative title) may provide similar facilities for the creation of disruptive pupils. This applies more particularly to full-time, semi-permanent provision than to specialised help in the ordinary classroom. But where the segregation is rigid and the stigmatisation overt the possibility is that disruption across the whole school is as likely to be increased as diminished by such provision. Many pupils may prefer to attend such classes and some pupils may even benefit from them (though firm, long-term evidence for this has yet to be brought forward) yet they are likely to remain concentrations of disruptive behaviour. In some schools this may be accepted, the class or classes even being relegated outside the school building. In less isolated provisions their negative influence is likely to be mediated through the peer group. The artificial concentration of labelled and disaffected children is likely to be a focus for rule-breaking in the playground and in corridors; their anti-authority attitudes may be attractive to other adolescents, their examples of non-attendance and unpunctuality hold out an alternative colourful model of pupil life always available for peers to adopt. The argument here is not that such classes are a bad thing *per se* (that is a separate argument) but rather that on the whole they are as likely to facilitate disruption as to mitigate it.

Turning to more mundane administrative matters, corridor, playground and lunchtime arrangements may also encourage disruption. The old urban school architecture with its multitudes of unsupervised booming staircases is almost as much of an invitation to disruptive behaviour as modern, parsimoniously narrow corridors and flimsy building materials. Any of these features may facilitate disruption if too frequent lesson or room changes are time-tabled or if no teacher is taking responsibility for supervision. Such disruption concerns all teachers as it is likely to spill over into lessons through lateness and the continuation of an excited atmosphere. It has been suggested (Reynolds 1976a) that some kind of tacit arrangement is made between staff and pupils in those schools which do not suffer too much disruption. It may not then be best for all school space to be supervised at all times; pupils need some freedom to carry on their own activities, even if the activities of some will inevitably be nefarious. However, all school space needs to be supervised at some time and any potential miscreants swept on their sullen or back-chatting way. Rather than treating duties as a matter of sentry patrol, it may be possible, particularly in primary schools, to teach and develop positive play. Facilities need to be made available beyond the knockabout game of football which so often dominates huge swathes of playground; teachers and dinner ladies need to know how to initiate and encourage games, sport and conversation (see Hart Shea and Rowlands 1980). This, of course, would be much easier if teachers, flaming swords in hands, did not expel pupils from the school doors three times a day. Making rooms and facilities available to children during breaks encourages responsibility and allows those who prefer studious or conversational forms of relaxation to exercise this preference. This applies to primary as well as to secondary schools; a warm, quiet hall with books and toys and some supervision can provide a necessary refuge from playgrounds too often perceived as hostile, boring or windswept. It is possible at both levels, too, to train and encourage dinner ladies to play a positive and directive role. Where school meals themselves present problems, they may perhaps be reduced if staff eat with pupils: lunchtime conversation with the children can prove a mutually relaxing and educative experience. Nearly all these suggestions have one thing in common besides their bright hopefulness: they involve teacher time. Help, space and equipment can all assist but ultimately behaviour at playtimes is likely to depend on teacher leadership, supervision and example. This can only be a popular proposal if teachers' commitments and exertions are properly recognised. An alternative is to shorten the school day. It is best for breaks and lunchtime not to be too long anyway, but where these have seemed to present an intractable problem, some local education authorities have allowed schools to cut them to a minimum so that education finishes at lunchtimes. This is a desperate measure though it may be effective: it is a movement back towards the fortress school rather than towards the interpenetration of school and community.

The ideal and practice of the community school might serve to discourage the creation of the disruptive pupil. Where children have access to staff and facilities at breaktimes, in the evenings and at weekends, there is less likelihood that anti-educational attitudes will develop. Teachers who run school teams or clubs or who work in adjacent youth centres may find that contacts developed outside the classroom assist in keeping lessons on a positive course. The arguments in favour of community education are far wider than this (see Fletcher and Thompson 1980), but where there is some commitment by teachers to more than the purely academic needs of their pupils there is likely to be less classroom disruption than in those schools where teachers motor away at four o'clock to leafier areas.

Contact with parents as partners in educating their children is also likely to be helpful. Where parents are encouraged to come into the school and given positive – not necessarily ancillary – roles, where they are given the opportunity to use the facilities and expertise of the school, where, above all, they are involved in an equal and active dialogue on the education of their children, the result will be to reduce disruption. It is worth emphasising that this demands an entirely different stance on the part of teachers from blaming parents for pupils' disruptive behaviour, from pulling them into the head's office after a particularly stormy episode in the hope that tongue-lashing them will prove more effective than tongue-lashing their offspring. In such parental 'interviews' the values of the school and home are

brought into sharp opposition, and even if the parents are prepared to wave a stick for the school this may well lead to absenteeism rather than reformation. Certainly parents may be made
aware of events at school but such contact can be positive as well
as negative: if letters were sent home about good work and
behaviour, if parents were invited to school to hear when children were progressing well, perhaps any comments about misbehaviour might meet with more than sullen resentment or mutual
blame. But this involves more than termly reports and annual
parents' evenings; it means a reciprocal dialogue in which the
participants meet face to face and in which teachers take notice of
what parents say as well as vice versa.

Finally, the ability on the part of a staff to accept assistance
may help minimise disruption. This assistance can come from
within the school as well as outside. Classroom disruption does
place teachers, particularly the inexperienced, under stress: they
may need opportunities to talk this through, guidance and advice
and sometimes active tangible assistance. In many schools this is
provided by experienced colleagues acting as teacher-tutors or
running induction courses where these issues can be dealt with in
group discussion. Courses or department meetings may provide
help for more experienced teachers who still have difficulties and
for senior teachers who may become exhausted through supporting everyone else. Advisers, support teachers, psychologists and
even lecturers may provide help in the classroom which also
contains an element of training; they may be invited to run staff
groups or organise courses. In all this, however, there is perhaps a
paradox: it may be those teachers, or indeed schools, most in
need of help who, through unwillingness to reveal 'failure', are
least likely to ask for or accept support and advice. Where
classroom disruption is concerned even the most experienced
or brilliant teacher may come across perplexing difficulties.
Those who can share these difficulties and learn from each other
how to overcome them are least likely to create disruptive
pupils.

Peer group

Friends and peers are vital to the school life of children (Willis
1977: Corrigan 1979). The development of friendship and its
transactions through childhood and youth may often originate in
and centre on school. For older children school may provide a

chance to look at, talk to, display and show off in front of members of the opposite sex and to begin to make mature contact with them. The wider peer group provides an audience and a point of comparison and competition. Pupils may have very different priorities from the academic ones stressed by teachers: children go to school to see each other. The intricacies of pupil social life – chat, games, fights, pecking orders, initiation of sexual contact – provide a separate hidden curriculum for each school day through which emerge concepts of self and other people (Erikson 1968; Hargreaves 1972; Berger and Luckman 1971). Such concepts, of course, also depend on interaction in the family and indeed with teachers: but for the wider world, which the school at first represents, the peer group is of increasing importance. The emerging behaviour patterns of the child may be encouraged and reinforced by the praise, esteem, notice, laughter or even negative attention of the peer group. Some of these behaviour patterns may include disruptive classroom behaviour, though for the pupils concerned and for the peer group they are unlikely to be conceptualised in this way. In the short term a group can manipulate a pupil by a dare or victimisation to perform some action likely to lead to amusement, diversion or embarrassment. In the long term the manipulation may be less visible, involving repetition in different settings, but it is likely to encourage the development of stock classroom roles – the clown, the bully, the victim, the idiot, the one who argues cheekily with teacher, the tough guy, the glamour girl, the one who is really only interested in pop music/chess/comics. Obviously one does not accept these roles at their face value – indeed, part of a teacher's task may be to help children through them towards a more mature personality. Nevertheless, the reinforcement which pupils receive from acting out such roles in disruptive situations in class is one of the elements in school life which serves towards the creation of the disruptive pupil.

Unlike the other three aspects of school life discussed above, this one would seem to be less amenable to change by teachers. 'Why don't you leave those naughty, rough girls and come and sit on your own over here so you can work properly?' is an approach which seems both undesirable and counterproductive. Nevertheless, there are ways in which teachers can attempt to smooth out some of the harsh or negative aspects of peer group influence. The question of whether the practices of grouping in primary schools and streaming and setting at secondary level serve to develop a diversity of rich contact for pupils or rather to reinforce class/race/sex stereotypes (Cicourel and Kitsuse 1971) has been discussed above. But teachers could use grouping to encourage varied and positive contacts. Behaviour programmes which involve group monitoring or reward have also been mentioned above as potentially powerful procedures. With children of almost all ages, however, the teacher's most frequent and possibly most useful resource is discussion – with the individual, with the group as a whole or with the group apart from the individual. Such discussion needs skill, tolerance and the ability to withhold the adult view while children's own perceptions are emerging: for this reason it is sometimes rather portentously called counselling or group counselling (e.g. Hamblin 1974). The development of teacher skills in this area is likely to be useful, but if this leads to the professionalisation of conversation it can only restrict useful contact and lead to scepticism among colleagues.

The legitimations of the creation of the disruptive pupil

The wider legitimations of the creation of the disruptive pupil include educational psychology, the practice of special education, the professionalisation of disruptive units and the status of academic achievement. There is considerable overlap between these elements. The role of educational psychology (Potts 1982b; Swann 1982) involves both theory and practice: the theories are part of educational research at the highest level, which they almost seem to dominate; the practitioners, well versed in theory, have become institutionalised in senior posts in UK education authorities. This brief discussion will involve the role of the local authority educational psychologist and the influence of theory and practice on two conceptions – intelligence and behaviour – involved in the creation of the disruptive pupil. The fact that the practitioners appear to have a definite expertise beyond that of the teacher, usually validated by a university degree in what is called a science, means that they are people to whom heads, teachers, inspectors and administrators may turn for advice. Further, educational psychologists have replaced doctors as the gatekeepers to special education. This position gives them the power to remove from schools pupils whom, for one reason or another, teachers find undesirable. Carrying brief-cases full of tests, reminiscent of the black medical bag, often provided with luncheon vouchers and car allowances, paid appreciably more than most headteachers, called in for special conferences or away lecturing on courses, they are the embodiment of the high-status professional: their theories and advice are likely to be influential on schools, especially if they fit in with what teachers want to hear.

The concept of intelligence (Kamin 1974; Evans and Waites 1981) is of comparatively recent origin. It may be seen to rest on five linked ideas: that intelligence is a common factor which explains a person's performance over a wide range of mental activities; that this factor may be measured by intelligence tests; that this intelligence is subject to little change throughout a person's development; that it is largely a product of genetic endowment rather than of environment or education; that some racial groups, for this reason, have on average a higher intelligence than some others. Evans and Waites have shown that each step in this argument is highly questionable and Kamin has revealed several elements in Burt's data, on which the genetic theory of intelligence is still largely based, to be fraudulent. In the UK much of the status of educational psychologists and the apparently scientific techniques by which they select children for special education depends on their ability to administer IQ tests: a privilege from which the untrained are specifically prohibited. In the USA the sordid history of IQ testing perhaps entered its terminal phase with Judge Peckham's ruling of October 1979 against the Californian education authorities: '[The] defendants have utilised standardised intelligence tests that are racially and culturally biased, have a discriminatory impact against black children, and have not been validated for the purpose of essentially permanent placements of black children into educationally dead-end, isolated and stigmatising classes for the so-called educable mentally retarded' (Evans and Waites, p. 10). The controversy concerning the concept of intelligence needs to be examined in much greater detail than is possible here (see also Simon 1971) in order to understand the weaknesses of one of the major legitimisations of important school practices such as 11+ selection, streaming and special school segregation. These practices serve both to facilitate classroom disruption and to reify social judgements so that they become institutional categories. It may be that educational psychology's notion of intelligence and the paraphernalia of IQ tests do not meet the different needs of children but encourage the intolerance of those schools and teachers unwilling or unable to cope with anything but a small range of difference.

Educational psychologists' notions of behaviour are relevant both to the definition of classroom disruption and to the categorisation of children as disruptive and maladjusted. It has been shown (Bowman 1981) that since the 1944 Education Act, a safety valve has been provided for mainstream education by the mushrooming of schools for those perceived to be maladjusted. These schools have been used for the placement of children whose behaviour differs from that traditionally understood within the psychodynamic orientation to be maladjusted, but who do present apparently unacceptable problems of disruption in mainstream schools. Nevertheless, the places were still not sufficient or easily enough available, so the on- and off-site units, with their administrative advantages discussed above, were created. These have become outstanding examples of the use of the criterion of behaviour for legitimating separate and stigmatised education. Since educational psychologists validated this in the case of maladjusted placements with rhetoric drawn from psychoanalysis or behaviourism, they helped establish the educational practices and terminology within which a second category of stigmatisation – 'disruptive' – could be discovered.

The practices of special education facilitate the creation of the disruptive child because they provide an accepted precedent for the development of categorisations. Paradoxically the need for the new category may have arisen when teachers felt that special schools, despite their dramatic expansion since 1944, were not taking enough children considered to be problems out of the mainstream. Special schools institutionalise the criteria of intelligence and behaviour. The presence of existing institutions which categorically separate children on a semi-permanent, full-time basis, purely on the grounds of their perceived performance and/or behaviour provided a precedent and a model for the units. The processes of referral and assessment, for instance, adopted by many units may be seen as a diluted version of the procedures of special educational placement.

Similarly, the specialisation of expertise and the professionalisation of teachers in special education is a pattern which may be followed in the units. The units may tend to segregate teachers as much as pupils. Those teachers with the skills to minimise disruption in the mainstream classroom may be unable to transmit their knowledge by training and example to other teachers because they are institutionally separated from them. Teachers in the units, however, may not have these skills, being recruited perhaps from among those dissatisfied with mainstream schools and seeking an alternative. Certainly, as yet, these teachers are provided with little training, specialised help or supervision. The absence of headteacher or hierarchy limits the experience of those employed, prevents the development of structures of responsibility, and inhibits opportunities for promotion. The unit teachers, without adequate training, support or resources, yet dealing with children hand-picked for their potentiality to disrupt, may perhaps be in as unfortunate a position as their pupils. However, there are signs of developing professionalisation. The ILEA employs an advisory head and teachers for its disruptive pupils programme, and courses are run for their benefit. Nationally the development of NOISE (The National Organisation for Initiatives in Social Education)[1] gives further institutional validity to the units and to the disruptive child. If this group of teachers becomes professionalised, and if the units become satisfactory educational institutions (and some can claim to be as good as many schools), the category of the disruptive child will be further hardened by the investment in it of teachers' expertise and career prospects. Unfortunately, the professionalisation of the teachers of pupils perceived to be disruptive serves only to increase the likelihood of the creation of the disruptive child. What, after all, is the point of having special units and specifically skilled teachers if disruptive pupils cannot be found for them to process, remedy or contain?

The status of academic achievement is a social as well as an educational issue. It is linked to the notion of differential intelligence proselytised by educational psychology and now almost ubiquitously prevalent in the west. The rigid examination system at 16+ and 18+ in the UK reifies academic achievement and perceived individual intelligence differences. Certification is one of the mechanisms by which social stratification is reproduced (Bourdieu and Passeron 1977; Halsey *et al.* 1980). In secondary schools in particular there is, not surprisingly, a great stress on the courses that lead to qualifications. The pressure to publicise examination results suggests that it is on these grounds that parents are likely to choose schools for their children. Elements within the school which work against academic progress measured within the narrow terms of certification are likely to be viewed unfavourably. These elements are actually pupils who progress slowly at schoolwork or by their behaviour disrupt the course of lessons. Schools, following prevalent societal values, conceive their task as to educate those who can 'benefit' from lessons. Those who cannot benefit from education thus narrowly defined are, ergo, undesirable. The very stress on standards and excellence for one stratum of the school population serves to increase the likelihood of others being transformed into disruptive pupils.

This chapter has insisted that disruptive behaviour must be seen as the product of the interaction of various elements – pupil, peer group, teacher, school organisation – within a specific social context, and not as the inherent result of the character of one participant. In doing this it has tended to neglect the wider social and economic context. It has been suggested (Tomlinson 1981; Apple 1979) that the categorisation of children as having special needs or as being disruptive is part of the structural process of the reproduction of stratified labour power according to the demands of the capitalist economy. It has been pointed out, however, that there is some circularity in this argument with regard to special education, in that it tends to suggest that whatever institutions exist must perform a function necessary to the continuation of the status quo: 'Are ESN(M) schools and their associated categorisation procedures the social glue without which our world would fall apart?' (Booth 1982a). This is not, of course, directly to contradict the argument. Categorisation occurs on specific sites and through social processes and articulations which this chapter has attempted to examine. However, without an examination of specific instances, long-range reproduction theory may be as much a counsel of despair in the disrupted classrooms as deficit models of pupils' families.

Those teachers working with so-called disruptive pupils are at the most visible and blatant extreme of education for social control (see Whitty, Chapter 9 of this volume). If children see their peers whose progress or behaviour has been repeatedly criticised by teachers removed summarily to a disruptive class or unit, this is likely both to give them the impression that the teachers' comments are based on justifiable criteria which can be actualised into institutional placement, and to motivate them to conform to accepted educational standards of behaviour. The units function as a major force of social control not only for the pupils who have contact with them but for all children in the educational system. At the same time, if children perceived as difficult are removed schools need not evolve the curricula and pedagogy which might, with appropriate administrative change, have allowed them to remain with their peers. The fact that many radical, innovative and caring teachers also find their way into special schools and units also removes pressure on the mainstream to adapt. Ironically, such adaptations would be likely to benefit all children in terms of a more relevant and stimulating curriculum and a more caring and flexible administration and teaching style, for much of what has been recommended above, for instance, is surely little more than good educational practice. The children not relegated to the disruptive category are adversely affected in one further way. The separate education of the created disruptive pupils alongside that of all those perceived to have special needs serves to legitimate for both the hale and the halt a morbidly constrained ideal of normality, within which all the latter are perceived to be inferior. Both actual separation and the idea of radical difference continue into adult life with resulting limitations on the humanity of both parties.

Note

1 The National Organisation for Initiatives in Social Education was established in 1981 for teachers of disaffected pupils working mainly in special units or centres. Its principal aims were to provide a forum for the exchange of ideas and mutual support in the development of policies and expertise. The organisation has now broadened its scope and involves those dealing with social education in the mainstream of education as well as in agencies outside the school system.

8
Special units: some underlying issues

Mike Golby

Special units are by definition special. If they are to be justified as providing a distinctive service to particular and identified categories of pupils, they must offer an educational environment significantly different from that which those pupils would otherwise experience. It follows from this fundamental statement that such significant differences as are built into the design of special units should be intelligible against a fundamental rationale or philosophy of education. It is my contention that too little attention has been given to the formulation of these fundamental educational issues. This is the case not only in relation to special units but also in many other contexts of curriculum and institutional development. However, the phenomenon of the special unit presents us with a new and challenging example of the need to articulate an innovation alongside a clarification of fundamental aims and purposes. My own interest in special units is not confined to, neither does it originate from, a compassionate regard for pupils with special difficulties. Neither have I any full-blown convictions about the best way forward whether for a particular type of pupil or for schools considering their own experience with difficult pupils. Indeed, the range of choice among so many convictions and so many enthusiasms working in so many different directions is bewildering.

It seems that while there is no shortage of working models, ideas and ideals in the special unit field, what is in short supply is clarity of vision and principle for the establishment, development (or indeed discontinuation) of special units inside the educational system at large. We must assume that we have an educational system which aspires to be comprehensive and egalitarian and to deliver the maximum satisfaction to all its clientele. Moreover, the clientele of the system must be regarded not only as individual pupils, but also as their parents and society at large. Education is a social investment in the rising generation, an investment in social and cultural continuity and change. The system we have has developed historically over a very long period of time and on assumptions which, while valid historically, may have little relevance to today's situations. Thus the educational system rests upon a kaleidoscope of values and assumptions and lacks a coherent and modern overall rationale. Nowhere is this clearer than in the comprehensive school where post-elementary, grammar and comprehensive ideals are in chronic conflict. If special units are to be more than merely local expedients and responses to the most obvious and strident demands on the schools then policy questions surrounding their existence must be addressed, made explicit and debated. I do not say here that such questions must be 'resolved' because I suspect and fear that there are indeed unresolvable contradictions among the many sincerely held views and skilfully executed practices in units. These contradictions emanate from ideological conflicts between assumptions and values hardened into the system like geological strata at the various stages of its evolution.

Since education is a branch of social policy its controversies should be as fully expressed as possible, not only for the sake of the pupils themselves, their parents and teachers, but also because there is a special obligation on educationists to face and share their dilemmas with a wider public. For education, more than any other social service, has the specific characteristic that it is concerned with the quality of the whole of a person's life and not merely with, say his bodily or mental health, his vocational skills or social adjustments. In considering special units we should at the same time be engaging in a social dialogue incorporating as many voices in the debate as possible. It is the purpose of books such as this to raise the level of debate and orientate it towards the most crucial and important questions.

It follows that the sort of discussions necessary to back up policy development in the special unit field will necessarily draw upon a wide range of social thinking. I stress the social nature of such thinking, and indeed its political implications, simply because it seems to me that much of the literature has a tendency to regard difficult children as individual psychological 'problems'. There is of course a unique and individual aspect to these questions in as much as children must be considered as individuals and dealt with on a personal basis. Nevertheless, pupils must always be grouped for practical purposes and their education undertaken within an institutional context. This being so, there will always be a social, and political, aspect to the decisions we take in relation to curriculum and institutional development. There is a connection between the purely psychological or individualistic modes of thinking about difficult pupils and the tendency to *ad hoc* solutions. An accumulation of temporary expediencies may amount to a policy, and perhaps policy has to emerge from experiment; but there is a need to consider the social context in a more rounded way. Thus I wish to connect the social dimension of the question of special units with the necessity to debate their place within the whole educational provision made for *all* pupils. The fact that small special units are invariably more expensive per head than conventional educational provision is only the financial side of an ideological question. In these days of stringency it is perhaps the most striking feature of the situation. In the longer term, however, the assumptions we make as to what constitutes a special pupil and what is appropriate to his development will inevitably be equally significant. It is my purpose to indicate a number of the forms of thinking which seem to underlie some of the practice in the field in the hope that others may find a framework or at least a starting point for discussion.

The most obvious starting point is to locate the problem of the difficult pupil in the pupil himself. Individualistic explanations may take the form that the pupil is *wilfully* disobedient or disruptive; in this case the pupil is accorded free will and regarded as a chooser who must be shown or made to see the error of his ways. Alternatively, he may be regarded as in some more or less deep way confused, so that he cannot make the right choices; he disobeys and disrupts because of some personal need, perhaps for attention, self-esteem or misplaced satisfaction.

The first explanation utilises a legal model casting the pupil as self-controlled and, therefore, a suitable case for rational discussion or explanation and for punishment since he or she has willingly chosen a false path. The second explanation invokes a medical model and sees the pupil as a suitable case for treatment or therapy.

Although there may not always be a strict distinction here in terms of diagnosis and school procedures, there is an ultimate set of questions surrounding all practice in dealing with individual miscreants. To what extent is the client responsible for what he has done and will do? How can he be made more responsible? If responsible, to what extent are we therefore committed to rational or quasi-rational forms of treatment, such as explanation, discussion and analysis? To what extent is therapy, in its many forms, an appropriate response to wilful and responsible behaviour? To what extent is punishment appropriate? And what about 'behaviour modification' which is akin to punishment in being an attempt to shape a pupil's overt behaviour though without necessarily recoursing to principled discussion. These are deep philosophical questions, but the lines of debate are tolerably clear and the questions for the practitioner perhaps defined in at least a preliminary sort of way. What should also be clear is that both forms of individualistic explanation share an assumption that the fabric of rules and expectations against which the pupil has been judged is itself right. It is as if there *is* some straightforward normative moral and institutional condition that all pupils will conform to providing they are aware of it and in control of themselves. The obvious analogy is with the concept of physical health, though there are difficulties even here (does health include levels of functioning or 'fitness' which extend beyond the absence of disease, 'fitness' to do what?). Because of this superficial similarity with health, the idea of a 'medical model' is sometimes deployed at this level of individualistic explanation in what I have called its second form. It is a doubly superficial similarity whilst concepts like community and family medicine are being developed, since these ideas stress the social nature of much individual malaise.

While the legal model differs from this in its stress on rules, obedience, judgement and punishment, it is similar in that it too provides an individualistic explanation. Both models locate the problems within the individual child and both assume the rectitude of the child's social environment. The pupil as patient or law-breaker, however, is not fully described for he is also to be seen as a member of a family and much attention has been given to the familial context in the recent past.

The home deficit theory

The idea that the quality of home life is a crucial determinant of school success is both popular with teachers and backed by a long line of speculative and research evidence. Much of the professional literature is uni-directional in suggesting that the whole problem is one of enlisting the home in the pursuit of school goals and in that way taking for granted the appropriateness of the school and its curriculum. There is no doubt, however, that in regard to many of the pupils who cause the most obvious concern in schools there is a family factor at work. West and Farringdon (1973) found that behaviour disorders due to personal and family factors – low ability, poor self-image, family violence and criminality, poverty, inadequate housing, growing up in a large family, inconsistent parental discipline and frequent prolonged absence of the father during the pupil's adolescence – were the main elements linked with violence and disruption. Millham *et al.* (1976) found that differences between standards and methods of punishment used by the family and the school could lead a pupil to reject school discipline. Mays (cited in Rutter and Madge 1976) found a similar link when differences existed between the standards of behaviour condoned by the community within the school's catchment area and those expected by the school.

A practising headmaster (Marland 1977) broadens the causes and adds an interesting insight of his own:

> You can't simply say it's all due to single parent families or immigrant backgrounds or overcrowding or broken homes – it's remarkable how many children from these backgrounds lead normal lives. But there does seem to be a correlation between family non-communication and violent behaviour in school. If there has been a gradual breakdown of love and trust between the family, because of a long drawn out illness or divorce, the child cannot cope. To be brutally objective, a quick death or a rapid divorce appears to be infinitely less harmful. The result of this discord is that parents and child lose touch, the child fails to learn to cope with his emotions and he reacts to frustration with aggression because he knows no other way.

So much is widely agreed. In respect of some of the extremes of difficulty experienced by pupils stemming from adverse home circumstances there may be very little that the school can do. Education cannot compensate for such dire straits, though schools could co-operate more fully with other agencies more directly charged with immediate care. This leads us to consider the suggestion that schools may themselves be contributing to the problems of their difficult pupils.

The institutional level

A school as a social system seeks certain sorts of aims and values certain types of success. Could it be that there is an arbitrariness and an inappropriateness about these aims and values for very many children? Could it be that the least tractable pupils represent merely the most expressive of the large numbers of the disaffected? This line of thinking is better represented in the sociological literature than in the minds of teachers, perhaps for the very good reason that no career teacher can really afford to entertain the view that the school is not at least nearly right in what it sets out to do, whatever the messiness of practice. It is, however, a view we must consider seriously if we are to see specialised arrangements for specified groups of pupils in the context of the value system of the whole school.

Part of the problem with this viewpoint may be academic elitism, part an over-emphasis on competition; part may be due to the organisation, conduct and atmosphere of the school.

> For many years we have tended to concentrate upon a minority of the more academically able children; we have stressed and probably exaggerated ability to pass routinised examinations and seriously undervalued moral and aesthetic development. One outcome of this process has been to divide society into potentially hostile camps of the more and the least successful people, facing each other with mutual incomprehension and aversion. Such social cultures provide seed beds and forcing ground for delinquency and maladjustment, for social isolation and despair. (Mays 1973)

There is some research which supports the sort of thinking propounded by Mays. Pringle (1973) links violent and disruptive behaviour with a curriculum which places too little emphasis on individual non-academic achievement and too much on competition. Hargreaves (cited in Rutter and Madge 1976) concurs with Pringle and maintains that in such schools pupils unable to achieve academic distinction turn to bullying and disruption as a way of gaining attention and status; and that streaming aggravates this situation. Rutter (1979) found that differences between schools with high and low delinquency rates were due to factors connected with the school itself as well as to the home environment. He discovered that some schools seemed to succeed in reducing pupils' delinquency while a few seemed to produce a higher delinquency rate. Reynolds' (1978) research in a small number of Welsh schools had led to similar conclusions. He argues that aspects of the education system in general and particular aspects of certain schools within that system actively function not to prevent delinquency but to create it. Whilst he accepts that pupils from disadvantaged homes are at higher risk of educational failure he is anxious to express his belief that the 'conventional explaining away' of pupils' problems as caused by internal personality disorders, family malfunctioning or parental effects on their children's development is inadequate.

At the institutional level we encounter a rather difficult set of issues. Unquestionably, schools, like families, clubs and societies, define their own criteria of success. Success, of course, implies failure; but how unjust and arbitrary are the academic and behavioural standards of the schools? To answer such a question will require a full analysis of our conception of the aims of schooling. It will have to be sufficient here only to note that specialised provision for difficult pupils will reflect assumptions in this area. At times a special unit will be seen as a bastion of support to the values of the mainstream; at other times dissenting views may find expression in the marginal territory of a unit.

The societal level

School values must be seen against a social context; pupils are members of a wider society as well as of the school. The tendency here is to point to very large-scale changes in social conditions, and increases in the rate of change. A good example of this sort of thinking is Rust (1977). She argues that most authorities in the western world, from nation states to family groups, are undergoing challenges to their sovereignty at present, and sees no reason why schools should be exempt from this. She sees anger and defiance in primary and secondary schools and disruption in universities as evidence of conflict of thought and values, and of institutional malfunctioning; she argues that whilst some nations are struggling into 'modernity', the 'post-modern' nation states in the western world are going through another social and cultural revolution in which the former modern-age assumptions are becoming increasingly unacceptable. Rust's analysis is that the process of 'modernity' involves industrial, commercial, economic, political, intellectual and psychic change. This social and cultural transformation has been so slow in the west that the fundamental and revolutionary changes which it has necessarily entailed have been masked; but each of the dimensions of 'modernity' mentioned above has reached crisis point in 'mature' or 'post-modern' states, particularly in America.

Rust regards education as one of the variables, along with urbanisation, literacy, media and political participation, of the modernisation process; and outlines what she believes has happened to education as a result of political, scientific, and technological advances. Politically, she argues, all major systems have been school enforcers; but just as a coalescing of local and international forces is challenging the sovereignty and dominance of the nation state, so individual, community and cultural forces are challenging the sovereignty and dominating methods of state schooling. Scientifically, says Rust, in 'post-modernity' there is a reaction against the rigidity of some scientific training which has ill prepared some scientists to cope with the scientific revolutions that have occurred, with the result that human beings have tended to be seen as expendable organisms. This has contributed to a process of dehumanisation and depersonalisation which has undermined man's sense of self in various ways; and this is no longer acceptable in society or in our schools.

Modern technological society with its nuclear power, electronic developments and automated production processes has created standardisations which have further contributed to dehumanisation and depersonalisation. Technology may be defined as the systematic application of knowledge to accomplish some goal.

It arrived on the American educational scene in the form of 'educational efficiency experts', 'human engineers' and a vast range of mechanical teaching aids. This technology of maximum efficiency became elevated in society and in schools to the realms of ideology. 'Know-how' and efficiency seemed to take on ultimate value to the extent that they emancipated themselves from human control. The 'post-modern' world reacts to this by asking such questions as 'everything may be running smoothly but what worthwhile is being accomplished?' 'What are the inbuilt costs of this efficiency?' 'Why have we allowed technology to rationalise away enormous areas of freedom in our lives?'

Such are the forces and reactions that Rust sees at work in 'modern' and 'post-modern' society and in our schools.

In referring briefly to Rust's analysis as an example of theorising at the societal level we are not of course suggesting that pupils are aware of the precise components of these changes. If we were to believe that in some direct way a perception of these large social changes was a factor in the school difficulties of specific groups of pupils, we would have also to believe that the least educationally successful pupils were the most percipient sociologists and cultural analysts among the young. Such theorising as Rust's is tempting, as are generalisations about compulsory schooling in a permissive society, but as a rule they fail to explain why certain groups of pupils have the particular difficulties they do have. Quite possibly it would be better to adopt an empirical approach in an attempt to understand the 'life-world' of specific pupils in particular schools. What interests them and what does not? What are their physical circumstances in regard to housing and clothing, for instance? What is their capacity for friendship? How do they conceive their prospects in the world of work? What is their understanding of their potential as parents and citizens? To address questions such as these would take us in and out of the various levels identified above; it would be a painstaking task requiring special conditions not found in the standard comprehensive school classroom; it would be the kind of task that many teachers believe they are in teaching to undertake. If a special unit makes a conscientious and half successful attempt in these directions we shall have to ask, if it can work with those particular pupils what about that other great majority, their peers?

It is clear, then, that there is no general agreement on the precipitating causes of disturbed and disturbing behaviour in comprehensive schools any more than there is a consensus on the best form which solutions to the problems arising from such behaviour should take. Both diagnosis and prescription are functions of pre-existing belief systems. I have tried to sketch some of the key dimensions of such beliefs and further conceptual work should proceed in the context of concrete examples. Whatever the underlying causes, however, recognition of the fact that there are problems became more widespread throughout the seventies and this led to experiments both outside and inside state school systems.

The experimental units which are the special object of study in this book are in something of an educational limbo in this country at present, even though it could be argued that their very existence and proliferation seem to indicate that they are meeting certain contemporary needs. Reservations about the development of special units centre, firstly, on doubts whether the needs they meet are those of pupils, teachers, schools, or society in general; and on whether schools can be expected to accept responsibility for meeting such a range of needs. There are many instances among the statements recorded in research into units in which worries are expressed about the width of the unit teacher's role which encompasses parental and social service functions alongside that of teaching. Secondly, there is a natural suspicion that units might foster bad as well as good practice; what goes on in them is even less publicly accessible than what goes on in the main school and much less easily accounted for and controlled. Such cautions should not be too readily dismissed as bureaucratic or political machinations for there are important public policy issues involved here. At the very least, units should be developing ways of giving honest and convincing accounts of their work. The growth of units may then be seen as a response to be encouraged or as a reaction to be discouraged, a progressive or a reactionary step.

The most ardent advocates claim that units ought to be regarded as forerunners of emerging institutional change because they have successfully tackled some of the effects being felt in schools of what Rust (1977) calls the 'post-modern social and cultural revolution'. Unit teachers have achieved this by facing the conflict in thought and values which they found both in their pupils and within themselves; and in doing so have provided a functional setting for both groups whereas, as they were not slow to point out, the schools from which their pupils had been transferred, or from which they had truanted or had been excluded, appear to them to be malfunctioning as institutions. They claim, not without justification, that some units have been conceptualised and set up as places for pupils which the mainstream comprehensive schools have rejected because they could not cope with them; moreover unit pupils represent, in their view, merely the visible tip of an iceberg. Underneath the disruption and truancy, which have led to a sharp rise in suspension rates in a number of local education authorities in the past few years and have led some of them to set up units, lies a more comprehensive continuum of pupil defiance, disturbance, disaffection, disillusionment, boredom, underachievement, and lack of motivation to learn. Advocates of units declare that pupil rejection takes the form of apathy as well as of hostility.

In short, the ardent supporters of units see them as a cutting edge, a sort of conscience at work in the system which they hope will make for more general educational reform, both with regard to teaching methods (where more continuous contact with pupils appears a principal desideratum) and to curriculum (where 'relevance' brings in train local studies, careers education and remedial work in the basics).

On the other hand there are many who regard units as sinister because 'they are full of protesting teachers as well as protesting pupils' (an LEA administrator), and because 'teachers in units are merely colluding with the truants as did the deschoolers or they are engaging in an ego trip and thereby avoiding the reality of the situation in comprehensive schools as did the free schoolers' (an LEA adviser).

There are also charges of incoherence in the rationale for units:

> 'They abolish structures by claiming to be "non-authoritarian" which means that they have no authority, by being "non-directive" which means they have no sense of direction, and by being "non-judgemental" which means that they are incapable of making a judgement or a decision' (a headmaster of a comprehensive school which did not have a unit).

> 'I fear that they may be emphasising method at the expense of substance which may lead to a decline in the quality of teaching, although I am well aware that here in the main school we may have emphasised substance at the expense of method with the result that pupils who are not able to gain great intellectual achievement have become uninterested and unmotivated' (the headmaster of a comprehensive school with a unit).

The grains of truth underlying the statement of protagonists and antagonists alike require further investigation and thought, and contribute to the policy problem in educational development which units currently pose to educational decision makers. Units are a particular case of a general issue, that is, the desirability or otherwise of providing distinctive educational experience for defined categories of pupils; and there is room for much fuller investigation into such areas as the relationship between unit curricula and mainstream school curricula. We know that many units attempt to retain contact with the main curriculum. We ought to discover soon how successful these endeavours are. Equally, we need to know whether units are allowing some schools to 'consume their own smoke' by 'quarantining' the dissatisfied, or whether they allow some schools to avoid pressures for beneficial change by, for example, delaying a wider acquisition by teachers of the necessary classroom skills needed to cope with a comprehensive intake. My suggestion is that the case study method offers the prospect here of substantial insight into the way units are in fact working in specific situations. It is clearly not possible to foresee whether units will become a widely accepted part of the system in the way that mini-schools have become established in over half of the high schools of New York City; or whether units are forerunners in the sense that they and other alternatives (such as 'vocational' units or 'basic skills' units or performing art units) might become alternative options complementing the universal elements in a core curriculum. The concern for more choice in education currently emanating from certain political quarters might gain a new twist if parental choice were extended to alternative *forms* of education within the comprehensive system. Not only is the maximisation of choice official Conservative party policy; it is also a key plank in the platform of the Advisory Centre for Education, which reported in 1979 a very heavy preference among parents for choices of alternative types of secondary school.

A study of the diversities within other national educational systems where alternative forms of education are more readily available might provide a starting point in considering what range of choices might be possible within a comprehensive school system; or, more close to home, a careful study of what is educationally worthwhile in the units already in existence in this country.

In particular, to insert a final subjective and tentative pointer which arises from personal observations, it might be helpful to explore the variety of ways in which many units are placing the self-concepts of pupils and teachers at the heart of a learning/ teaching process which combines curriculum, pedagogy and therapeutic insights.

From this perspective it is the following features of work in units that impress:

1 The emphasis on rewards, rather than punishments, in that 'reinforcers' are used to motivate and promote learning and growth rather than merely to ensure control.
2 The flexible use of a variety of learning methods including individualised learning, group learning, peer learning, and resource based learning.
3 The consistent framework of discipline which involves the skills of knowing what to accept and what to challenge, when to accept and when to challenge, and how to accept and how to challenge; and which enables teachers to be in authority without being authoritarian, and ensures a general acceptance of what are the negotiable and non-negotiable areas between teachers and pupils.
4 The practical acknowledgment of the fact that self is present in all behaviour including learning and that one way of improving learning is to enhance the self concept. This appears in both individual and group counselling, and in the care taken to ensure that the goals of the units, the tasks assigned and the activities engaged in are personal and human rather than impersonal and institutional.
5 The ways in which the teachers have redefined and redesigned their roles to become skilled managers of pupils as well as skilled managers of content, communication and materials.

In short, many units now recognise the fact that there is 'a persistent and significant relationship between the self concept and academic achievement' (Purkey 1970). This may well lead to a reconceptualisation of the processes and relationships in the classroom, the teacher's role, the nature of learning, the curriculum and teaching methods, evaluation processes, and the general management system.

To see such units as forerunners or as bridges between the past and the future is both extravagant and pretentious; but might they not at least be seen as positive and helpful critics of comprehensive schooling?

9
Special units in a changing climate: agencies of change or control?

Geoff Whitty

In this chapter I shall attempt to place special units for disaffected pupils[1] in their changing sociological context and consider some of the implications of that analysis for policy and practice in this field. My major concern will be with off-site units, as, although on-site units often pose similar dilemmas, they do not do so in quite so stark a manner. It is perhaps wise to admit at the beginning of this chapter that my credentials for discussing special units are somewhat limited. My interest in them was initially aroused when teaching a course about alternatives to mainstream educational practice to PGCE students in the mid-1970s. This brought me into contact, both directly and indirectly, with a number of quite inspiring examples of alternative educational practice outside or on the fringes of the state educational system. Nevertheless, my instincts as a sociologist inclined me to regard such innovations as providing a safety-valve through which disruptive and alienated pupils could safely pass (often along with their non-conforming teachers), thus leaving the mainstream system unreformed to the continuing disadvantage of the mass of pupils who would never have the opportunity of entering such units whatever their educational value.

The need to try to come to terms with these contrasting perceptions of special units was made more urgent for me in the late 1970s by a number of occurrences. One of these was the presence within one of my higher degree classes of Roger White, whose own work on the ROSLA Project (White and Brockington 1978) and at the Bayswater Centre in Bristol (White 1980) was amongst the best in the field but whose conclusions about its broader educational and social significance seemed to me altogether more

suspect and sociologically somewhat naïve. Though he subsequently took on board some of the sociological analyses with
which I confronted him, White was to restate his central argument in the following terms:

> Even if we accept the validity of the sociological critique of
> schools, the question still remains unanswered about the
> most effective ways of changing the situation. It is too easy
> to get caught up in an ideological debate about the legiti-
> macy of such provision, when the possibilities for imple-
> menting change in the parent system are rather restricted.
> Whether these units are seen as a reasonable distribution of
> provision within a healthy status quo, or merely as cosmetic
> operations that disguise basic weaknesses and delay struc-
> tural reform, is largely irrelevant.
>
> What is important is what lessons they hold for general
> educational provision. The question to ask *now* is: what can
> we learn from the operation of those special units that might
> improve the provision within schools? They do offer an
> opportunity to test out experimental ideas, both in terms of
> form and content. Given the degree of commitment from
> those staffing them, they do present a unique chance to
> grasp innovative ideas and ideals. (White 1980)

However, other developments at this time made me even more
doubtful of the viability of White's optimistic model of educational change and his perception of the role of special units as
change agents for the mainstream system. One of these was the
increasing tendency for local educational authorities to start their
own special units rather than developing a working relationship
with the sort of semi-autonomous enterprises that White seemed
to be advocating. While, in some respects, this could be seen as a
hopeful granting of legitimacy to special unit work within the
mainstream system, some of the complexities and the contradictions involved in this sort of development were dramatically
brought home to me by my experiences as a member of the
governing body of an autonomous off-site unit during a period
when it was trying (unsuccessfully as it turned out) to negotiate a
working arrangement with its local education authority.

It was because dilemmas about autonomy and incorporation,
and the role of units as agencies of change or control, kept
recurring within these various contexts that I agreed to Roger
White's suggestion that I should air some of the issues involved to

an audience of special unit workers at a conference held at Bristol University in December 1980. The present chapter is a further elaboration of some of the points that I put forward for consideration at that conference.[2] That White himself should have suggested that the reflections of a sociologist might be of value to an audience largely composed of practitioners within the special unit field suggests that even he did not feel that sociological issues were *entirely* irrelevant, nor did he feel totally confident that special units, as they were then developing, were quite the force for change that he felt they could be. At one level, however, I would tend to agree that some sociological accounts of the nature of schooling in general, or of special units in particular, *are* largely irrelevant if they seem to claim that there is a simple answer to the question of whether schools or special units maintain the status quo or challenge it. What educational institutions are, and what they do or do not do, depends on many things – on what they are intended to do and how they are run on a day-to-day basis, of course, but also on the specific historical context or conjuncture in which they are operating and on how their work articulates with other elements of the educational system and society at large. Thus, in discussing some of the trends in special unit policy and practice, and attempting to assess their implications, I am not attempting to develop a general theory of the relationship between special units and the mainstream system but rather attempting to understand the dynamics of that relationship within the specific political, economic and ideological context in which we are working in the early 1980s. This seems to be a rather different context from the one in which work such as White's developed in the early and mid 1970s. The survival of White's approach, based as it is on a new concept of the 3Rs, as Responsibility, aRticulation and Relevance, seems a crucial test of his claims that units can be a force for change since it remains far more committed to its early goals than some of the currently more fashionable approaches to special unit work, whether of the behaviourist or psycho-therapeutic varieties. These other approaches seem much more clearly resigned, if not committed, to leaving the rest of the educational world – let alone anything wider – largely unaltered.

For White, and like-minded workers in the special units field, part of the attraction of the sort of off-site educational centres for truants and disruptive pupils which received LEA encouragement in the mid-1970s was that, in many respects, they seemed to offer the best of all worlds. They did not constitute an extreme libertarian or anarchistic opting out of the system, but – like many of the independent free schools which made a more complete break with it – they did serve to expose the limitations of mainstream state education and provide possible alternative models for it. While such units were certainly partly a safety-valve for the mainstream system, the links they retained with it made them, potentially at least, a force for change within it. They also provided a context within which to experiment in educating those pupils which the mainstream system had most overtly failed, without the staff being constantly distracted from this task by the problems of scraping around for charitable funding.[3] Although such projects and units were off-site, the main justification offered for this at that stage was that it removed children from the sort of institutional context which they associated with past failures (see White 1979). While many of the buildings used for these early projects therefore deliberately lacked the institutional ethos of the school, this was in many cases seen as a way of exploring how educational settings might be better organised, not merely within special units but in the mainstream system as well.

This is not to say that motives for the LEA funding and support of such units were straightforward or that tensions between different goals for the units were not rife even then, but at that stage the ideological rhetoric of the 1960s with its emphasis on 'caring' lingered on and, indeed, often predominated (see Hill 1979). Thus, although control was certainly on the agenda, it was very much in the form of 'soft control' rather than coercion. The rhetoric of support rather than punishment, therefore, provided the social space within which those special unit staff committed to more radical ends could relatively easily operate. Indeed, the staff of a number of the early LEA-established units themselves came out of the world of free schools and alternative education and an article in *The Times Educational Supplement* in 1977 on the demise of Barrowfield Free School and the rise of special units in Scotland, explicitly argued that

Much of the theory, and even more of the practice, of special units and intermediate treatment derives from the free school phenomenon. A visit to a special unit or intermediate treatment project confirms the suspicion that they are free schools in disguise. Many of those involved admit that it is, directly or indirectly, from free schools that they have learned their lessons. (MacBeath 1977)

Yet this same article did not celebrate this as a triumph of free school ideals within the mainstream system, but rather suggested that this incorporation was the beginning of the end of them.

Personally, I would not entirely accept that conclusion if it is meant to imply that such an outcome was absolutely inevitable. Indeed, it is at least arguable that some of those free school ideals are better fought for within institutions which are part of the mainstream system and have a real possibility of influencing it. On the other hand, there are certainly aspects of the current climate which give some credence to MacBeath's fear that many of the most important elements of the free school experience are being lost as 'the free school concept [is] refined and trimmed to meet the expectations of the system'. Even the bureaucratic procedures involved in gaining LEA support for autonomous projects (which is what MacBeath seems to advocate for Barrowfield) can lead those involved into difficult decisions and dangerous compromises which some groups have reluctantly accepted (e.g. Grunsell 1979) while others have felt it wise to resist (e.g. White Lion Street Free School 1976). But even where those involved in community-based projects are willing to make such compromises, it often seems to those involved that LEA procedures can effectively serve to stifle and frustrate – rather than give constructive support to – significant educational innovations. Those involved with the Riverside Truancy Project in Bath during 1980 felt that this happened in the lengthy and ultimately abortive negotiations with Avon County Council for support for a project which many local people, both within education and outside it, considered to be a particularly imaginative and successful experiment. As with the case of Barrowfield, it was difficult to understand why an authority – which, ironically, was at that time notorious for having made savage expenditure cuts – chose to establish new (and ultimately probably more expensive) arrangements to contain truancy and disruptive behaviour in Bath at the same time as refusing support to a cheap and proven experiment.[4]

In these circumstances, it becomes tempting to conclude that LEA support will only be forthcoming for those projects whose central commitment is towards control and the maintenance of the status quo. Yet, before we are too easily tempted into accepting a conspiracy theory, we have to remember that the very same Avon County Council involved in the Riverside affair gave its support to the ROSLA Project and the Bayswater Centre in Bristol – and continued to give it even in 1980 when the ideological climate no longer demanded that each authority had at least one such fashionable experiment on its books. Nevertheless, it does seem unlikely that Avon, or indeed many other LEAs, would fund such projects if they were starting now when there is a clear tendency even for off-site provision in this field to be LEA-initiated and professionally staffed by their own existing employees.

This should not, however, necessarily be seen as a retrograde development. Thus it is not so much the establishment of such LEA units, as their establishment within a particular ideological climate, which gives rise to severe reservations about the work they are intended to do and the sort of relationship which is developing between them and mainstream educational provision. In the current context, it seems to me that those who see off-site special units as a force for change will have to fight extremely hard against pressures of a very different variety which are more in evidence, or at least more consistently, coherently and vociferously argued, than they were in the days of the early experimental units. Indeed, it is arguable that, at that time, any solution to the problems of truancy and disruptive behaviour was seen as better than none. Thus, as Roger White (1980) says of the Bayswater Centre, the support that it received from the LEA arose partly at least because there was so little provision of any kind for dealing with 'vulnerable pupils'. Although Avon's establishment of a new Stage 5 unit[5] in Bath at the same time as refusing support to the Riverside Project is probably no evidence of a conspiracy, it is certainly a sign of the times.

Looking through the literature on special units coming out of LEAs in recent years, it would be difficult to claim that its character is any longer much influenced by the rhetoric or ideals of the free school movement, even in its more conservative and highly structured guises. Certainly, White's concept of an education based on the new 3Rs of Responsibility, aRticulation and Relevance (White 1980) does not seem central to its concerns. Nor, interestingly, does the literature show much interest in influencing, as opposed to protecting, mainstream education. Although the research carried out in 1978 amongst fifty-six local education authorities by Young *et al.* (1980) showed that most tried to emphasise the educational component and potential of the work of their units, closer inspection revealed that many of the units were in fact established for more punitive reasons. Even though an authority might present its aims as threefold – to offer relief to schools, to facilitate education for the pupils referred, and to act as a deterrent to mildly disruptive pupils still in school – it seems clear that the sense of urgency evident in many of the proposals produced by local authorities arose from the needs of the mainstream schools rather than the educational needs of the pupils extracted from them. In these circumstances, it was difficult to avoid the perception of units as 'dumping grounds' and places of punishment. Even in 1978, the dilemma that arose from 'the need to provide an educational regime within a structure which [was] itself a form of sanction' was sometimes being resolved in the punitive rather than the educative direction. Young *et al.* wrote that one local authority, and ironically one that had claimed that 'establishments that are penal in character' were outside the ambit of the relevant education sub-committee, had a working party on its provision for dealing with disruptive pupils which recommended that

> A unit should be established along the following lines: 'Such centres should be single-sex, inconvenient, uncomfortable and offer less freedom than normal schools. If the local centre fails to correct this hard core, large houses should be purchased around the county, each catering for about fifteen of these pupils. They should, in the panel's opinion, be sent away from home to these special centres and not allowed home at weekends, though it is appreciated that there are important legal implications to this.' It is clear from this description that in the minds of this group the transition has been made, in the off-site unit, from school to penal institution. (Young *et al.* 1980)

The thinking in this case was, then, that of the penal institution rather than of an educational one and, arguably, that of the backwoodsmen of the penal system at that. While the authors clearly regarded this as an extreme example, much of their other data also reveals an underlying emphasis on punishment and the need to protect the mainstream educational system from pollution. Subsequently, such thinking has gained an even wider legitimacy in the ideological climate that has accompanied the early years of the Thatcher government and the emergence of

Rhodes Boyson as a central figure in the development of education policy at national level. Thus, the emphasis on the concept of a caring community seems to have diminished in recent writings and, although the units are seen as a way of *protecting* the mainstream system from disintegration, there is now little evidence of the notion that work in special units should influence what goes on in the mainstream system in a *positive* manner. Separate off-site units which pre-figure the development of a separate form of education for the disaffected and allow mainstream educational provision to continue undisturbed bring to mind an implication in Hargreaves' work (1978) that disruptive pupils in secondary schools may at least do the bored, but silent, majority a favour by *forcing* schools to change their ways. The tendency to become a safety-valve for the system was always one of the strongest arguments against free schools, but most of them did at least try to develop educative alternatives to mainstream schooling rather than potentially penal ones which would leave the mainstream system undisturbed.[6]

However, what is perhaps more interesting and disturbing than the hopefully extreme example quoted from the work of Young *et al.* is the subtle shift in the vocabularies of motive even amongst those LEAs that do have at least something of a reputation for being amongst the more liberal and progressive education authorities. Take as an example the job description for a new unit being established in 1981 in one such authority, the ILEA. This unit is to be established in part of an old primary school, have a scale 4 teacher in charge, a deputy on scale 3 and two teachers on scale 2, together with a dinner assistant and a clerical assistant. Applicants for teaching posts are told that the establishment is to be of a 'highly structured and tightly controlled' nature. Now it seems to me that the expression 'highly structured and tightly controlled' is an interesting one in this context. The rhetoric of providing a 'structured environment' has been fairly typical of many of these units from the very early days and it is the sort of rhetoric which, because it is open to so many different interpretations, has commanded a wide spectrum of support. Certainly it did not exclude those from the less extreme wing of the free school movement. But the expression 'tightly controlled' conjures up an altogether different picture and might well suggest that the authority does not wish those teachers committed to more democratic and non-coercive ideals to apply for posts in the unit.

It is also possible to detect something of a shift on the part of this authority towards an acceptance of a *de facto* separation of special unit pupils from the mainstream system. Thus, despite its having fought long and hard battles with free schools on this very issue, the authority's commitment to returning special unit pupils to the mainstream system looks like becoming a rather rhetorical one, at least for fourth- and fifth-year pupils. The job description for the new unit states that these pupils are likely to stay in the unit 'somewhat longer' than the half term which is typical for younger pupils in the authority's other units, but still with a view to eventual reintegration. But another document from the ILEA (1980) states quite explicitly that 'the school reintegration objective of the [authority's] programme appears to be unrealistic for older pupils'. In these circumstances it is perhaps significant that the job description for the new unit for older pupils makes it sound like a separate and slightly spartan institution, with outside toilets – albeit of a 'well-built and acceptable standard'!

Similarly, in looking through the ILEA's first report on its monitoring study of its Support Centres Programme (ILEA 1980), it is interesting to note that detailed information about what actually went in its units was not considered a vital concern in the first phase of monitoring, though it is now to be looked at in more detail. The initial omission of this aspect in an authority more committed than most to offering curriculum support and advice to its teachers is itself somewhat puzzling, but more disturbing is the fact that the programme can apparently be declared a success (*The Times Educational Supplement* 1980) on the basis of statistical data on programme implementation, even though the report itself commented on a lack of evidence about the curriculum objectives and activities of the support centres themselves. This is particularly disturbing when some of the limited evidence that we have of the practice of special units, even on-site ones, suggests that an absence of an adequate educational rationale can lead to the construction of a 'pseudo-structure' to combat the pupils' perception of the pointlessness of the whole operation – summed up in the constant complaint 'They don't learn ya nuffin'.[7] Even within relatively progressive education authorities, then, there is some evidence that the major emphasis has become one of removing problems from mainstream schools rather than meeting the educational needs of the pupils in the units. It is therefore understandable why some groups have perceived units as instruments of social control and a far cry from the agencies of change envisaged by White (1980). This has, of course, been a particular concern of ethnic minority groups and of West Indian parents in particular. Even the conclusion of ILEA's 'Ethnic census of school support centres' (ILEA 1981) that any over-representation of black pupils in its units was 'much less extreme than some commentators had feared' did not entirely allay the earlier fears expressed by groups such as NAME (Francis 1980b), particularly in respect of some individual centres.[8]

There does, then, appear to have been something of a shift in the ideologies implicit within predominant modes of discourse about special units. Although a variety of ideologies and practices continues to co-exist, it seems that the past decade has seen some decline in the legitimacy granted to those ideologies represented by segment 1 of the model (Figure 1) and an increase in

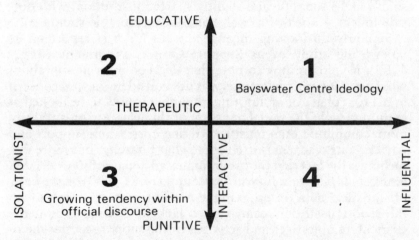

Figure 1 Special unit ideologies

that granted to those ideologies represented by segment 3. However, even the current economic and political climate is not completely monolithic. Even critical sociologists have come, in recent years, to recognise that the sorts of sociological critiques dismissed by White as largely irrelevant to the concerns of special unit practitioners failed to do complete justice to

the complexity of either school life, the actual and often contradictory conditions which tie education to an unequal society, or to the struggles and contradictions that exist in the school, the workplace ... in the State ... No assemblage of ideological practices and meanings and no set of social and economic arrangements can be totally monolithic. (Apple 1982)

Some policy initiatives, such as the Warnock Report and subsequent attempts to redefine the relationship of children with 'special educational needs' to the mainstream system contained contradictory elements, even if their less progressive features seem to be in the ascendancy at the present time (Barton and Tomlinson 1981). Meanwhile, a few LEAs deliberately choose to pursue relatively progressive policies against the trends outlined here.[9] Equally, there is clearly no one-to-one correspondence between policy priorities and what actually happens on the ground, and there is no doubt that some work that is quite consistent with White's ideals is still being carried on. However, such work is becoming increasingly marginalised by the emergent ideology of the newer units and this process makes its role as an agent of change much more difficult, particularly if the new-style units and their tendency towards isolationism paradoxically gain acceptance from mainstream educational provision. In these circumstances, the relationship between all units and mainstream educational provision, in both institutional and curricular terms, becomes crucial. In the current climate, the maintenance of 'distance' could unwittingly lend support to the reactionary versions of separatism now gaining official favour. Whatever the reservations of unit workers with a free school background, the recent trends in policy for special units which enhance a separateness that is potentially penal and custodial in character, rather than educational, make the maintenance of a close connection with the mainstream system of education even more vital than before.[10] Only thus are many units likely to retain an educational emphasis themselves, let alone influence educational practice in the mainstream system in the positive way envisaged by White. Indeed, some elements of the very system from which the early experimenters sought to escape may well be preferable to the more blatantly custodial ethos implied by some recent official initiatives, though this is certainly not to suggest that contemporary mainstream provision should in any way be viewed uncritically.

What is clear is that in the present political and ideological climate, those committed to the sorts of ideals espoused by White and his co-workers at the Bayswater Centre will have to become far better organised to defend what they are doing and to promote its extension than they have had to be in the past. The individualistic initiatives of the 1970s are unlikely to prove sufficient to command support in the very different ideological climate of the 1980s. White (1980) describes quite vividly the struggles, the isolation and the weariness involved in getting the Bayswater Project going, many of its early difficulties arising from its lack of resources. Ironically, when (despite the general economic climate) resources for some types of units suddenly seem to have become relatively abundant, the struggle to retain the ideology of a project like the Bayswater Centre will almost certainly become heightened. This does not mean that it is impossible to develop ways of defending and promoting its ideas that are appropriate to this new climate and there is evidence in the establishment of NOISE[11] that a start has been made in recognising the need to mobilise politically in support of the more progressive features of special unit work. Yet, as Ling (1982) points out, even here there is a danger of encouraging a separatist conception of special units rather than carrying the debate about the nature of provision within the whole system into contexts where mainstream policymakers and practitioners will have to listen. Thus, however NOISE conceives of its short-term defensive task in relation to progressive practice in existing units, it will certainly need to bear in mind the view of Eric Bolton, a senior HMI, that

> in the long run, more success may well be achieved by seeking to influence the major educational debates about the curriculum, examinations and pupil profiles than through a concentration on yet more types of alternative special provision for difficult pupils (Bolton 1981).

Notes

1　The terminology for describing these units and their clientele raises contentious issues. I use the term 'disaffected' pupils here to include both truants and 'disruptive' pupils. It is arguable that, alongside the changing ideologies of special unit work charted in this chapter, there has been a shift of emphasis from providing facilities for non-attenders at mainstream schools towards dealing with those pupils who disrupt mainstream provision. However, although some units do concentrate on one category of pupil rather than the other, many others provide facilities for both.

2 The conference, entitled 'The lessons of truancy' was held at the University of Bristol on 2 December 1980. My own paper, entitled 'Special units – a force for change or control?', was subsequently published along with other conference contributions in the *Journal for Workers in Social Education Centres*, no. 1, June 1981.

3 This was a recurrent experience for the workers at the White Lion Street Free School in Islington, London, who for many years chose not to accept local education authority finance because of the conditions attached to it (White Lion Street Free School, 1976). However, since this chapter was written, the school has come to a mutually satisfactory agreement with the new leadership of the ILEA, perhaps further evidence of the contradictory tendencies mentioned in this paper. See *The Guardian*, 15 September 1982.

4 My own interpretation of these events is disputed by the local education authority, but officers declined to make available to me the information which they claim would lead me to change my view were I to have access to it.

5 Stage 5 refers to a stage in the authority's standard disciplinary and suspension procedures.

6 A penal ideology is also evident in a confidential report to Dudley Education Committee, details of which were reported in *The Guardian* on 25 January 1982, under the headline ' "Isolation classes" plan to combat school violence'.

7 These comments draw upon research being carried out by Julian Wood at the University of London Institute of Education, and I am grateful for his permission to make use of it. Concerns about curricular provision in special units were also expressed at the Schools Council seminar on the needs of disruptive pupils held at Stoke Rochford in September 1980 (Evans, 1981).

8 See the article 'Disruptive or Disaffected?' in *Issues in Race and Education*, no. 34, Autumn 1981. *Issues* is produced by a group of London-based NAME (National Association for Multi-racial Education) members.

9 In view of this, it will be interesting to see how far the change of political control on Avon County Council and the emergence of a new left-wing leadership in the ILEA will lead to alterations in the policies discussed earlier in this chapter which was written before these developments took place.

10 In this connection, it is clear that many of those working in separate provision recognise the dangers. Thus the London Educational Alternatives Programme (LEAP) exists to help those who work 'in educational provision outside conventional schools, and who are committed to developing alternative models of education *with the*

aim of influencing mainstream schooling' (Peacey 1982, my emphasis).

11 NOISE is the National Organisation for Initiatives in Social Education, which developed out of the Bristol Conference mentioned in note 2 above. Amongst its aims, it seeks to 'encourage a continuing dialogue and the formation of practical links between centres, mainstream schooling and other relevant agencies' and 'to influence the formulation of both national and local policy with respect to the education of disaffected young people'. At the same time, it seeks to 'pool and disseminate information and to support the development of local initiatives' and to 'promote the professional standing and career structure for workers in ... centres' (NOISE 1982). The tension between these aims is presumably the basis of Ling's note of reservation (Ling 1982).

References

ADVISORY CENTRE FOR EDUCATION (1980) Disruptive Units – ACE Survey', *Where*, no. 158

APPLE, M. A. (1979) *Ideology and Curriculum* (London: Routledge & Kegan Paul)

APPLE, M. (ed.) (1982) *Cultural and Economic Reproduction in Education* (London: Routledge & Kegan Paul)

ASSOCIATION OF HEADMISTRESSES (1973) *Towards Adjustment* (London: AHM)

BARTON, L. & TOMLINSON, S. (eds) (1981) *Special Education: Policy, Practices and Social Issues* (London: Harper & Row)

BECKER, H. S. (1952) 'Social class variations in the teacher-pupil relationship', *Journal of Educational Sociology*, vol. 25, pp. 451–65

BECKER, H. S. (1963) *Outsiders: Studies in the Sociology of Deviance* (New York: Free Press)

BERGER, P. L. & LUCKMAN, T. (1971) *The Social Construction of Reality* (Harmondsworth: Penguin)

BERNSTEIN, B. (1971) 'On the Classification and Framing of Knowledge' in Young, M. F. D. (ed.) (1971) *Knowledge and Control* (London: Collier Macmillan)

BERNSTEIN, B. (1975) Class, Codes and Control: vol. III, *Towards a Theory of Educational Transmissions* (London: Routledge & Kegan Paul)

BIRD, C., CHESSUM, R., FURLONG, J. & JOHNSON, D. (1980) *Disaffected Pupils* (London: Brunel University)

BOLTON, E. (1981) 'Disruptive Pupils' in Evans, M. (1981) q.v.

BOOTH, T. (1981) 'Demystifying Integration', in Swann, W. (ed.) (1981) q.v.

BOOTH, T. (1982a) *Handicap is Social* (Milton Keynes: Open University Press)

BOOTH, T. (1982b) *Special Biographies* (Milton Keynes: Open University Press)

BOOTH, T. & STATHAM, J. (1982) *The Nature of Special Education* (Milton Keynes: Open University Press)

BOURDIEU, P. & PASSERON, J. C. (1977) *Reproduction in Education, Society and Culture* (London: Sage)

BOWLES, S. & GINTIS, H. (1976) *Schooling in Capitalist America* (New York: Basic Books)

BOWMAN, I. (1981) 'Maladjustment: a history of the category', in Swann, W. (ed.) (1981) q.v.

BOX, S. (1977) 'Hyperactivity – the Scandalous Silence', *New Society*, 1 December 1977

BRENNAN, W. (1982) *Changing Special Education* (Milton Keynes: Open University Press)

BRIGGS, D. & STATHAM, J. (1982) 'The Referral Process: Daniel and Harriet', in Booth, T. and Statham, J. (1980) q.v.

BRITISH ASSOCIATION OF SOCIAL WORKERS (1977) *Children Excluded from School* (London: BASW)

CASTLES, S. & WUSTENBERG, W. (1979) *The Education of the Future* (London: Pluto Press)

CHALK, J. (1975) 'Sanctuary Units in Primary Schools', *Special Education – Forward Trends*, vol. 2, no. 4

CHAZAN, M., LAING, A., SHACKLETON BAILEY, M. & JONES, G. (1980) *Some of our Children* (London: Open Books)

CICOUREL, A. V. & KITSUSE, J. I. (1971) 'The social organisation of the high school and deviant adolescent careers', in Cosin, B. R. *et al.* (eds) (1971) *School and Society* (London: Routledge & Kegan Paul)

COARD, B. (1977) 'What the British school system does to the black child', in Raynor, J. and Harris, E. (eds) (1977) *Schooling in the City* (London: Ward Lock)

COLLINS, J. (1982) 'Never Mind the Theory', *The Times Educational Supplement*, 10 September 1982, no. 3454

CORRIGAN, P. (1979) *Schooling the Smash Street Kids* (London: Macmillan)

CRAFT, M. (1966) 'Teaching and Social Work', *New Society*, 20 October 1966

CRAFT, M. (1967) 'Education and Social Work', in Pedley, R. (ed.) *Education and Social Work* (Oxford: Pegamon Press)

CRAFT, M. (1980) 'School Welfare Roles and Networks', in Craft, M. *et al.* (eds) (1980) q.v.

CRAFT, M., RAYNOR, J. & COHEN, L. (eds) (1980) *Linking Home and School* (3rd edn) (London: Harper & Row)

CUMBRIA EDUCATION DEPARTMENT (1976) *No Small Change* (Carlisle: Cumbria Education Department)

DANIELS, H. (1979) 'Disaffected 15- and 16-Year-Olds in a Comprehensive School', *Therapeutic Education*, vol. 7, no. 2

DAWSON, R. (1980) *Special Provision for Disturbed Pupils: A Survey* (London: Macmillan)

DES (1978a) *Special Educational Needs* (The Warnock Report) (London: HMSO)

DES (1978b) *Behavioural Units: a survey of special units for pupils with behavioural problems* (London: HMSO)

DES (1978c) *Truancy and Behavioural Problems in some Urban Schools* (London: DES)

ERIKSON, K. (1964) 'Notes on the Sociology of Deviance', in Becker, H. S. (ed.) (1964) *The Other Side* (New York: Free Press)

ERIKSON, E. H. (1968) *Identity, Youth and Crisis* (New York: Norton)

EVANS, B. & WAITES, B. (1981) *IQ and Mental Testing* (London: Macmillan)

EVANS, M. (1981) *Disruptive Pupils* (London: Schools Council)

FIELD, F. (ed.) (1977) *Education and the Urban Crisis* (London: Routledge & Kegan Paul)

FITZHERBERT, K. (1980) 'Strategies for Prevention', in Craft, M., Raynor, J. & Cohen, L. (eds) (1980) q.v.

FLETCHER, C. & THOMPSON, N. (eds) (1980) *Issues in Community Education* (London: Falmer)

FORD, J., MONGON, D. & WHELAN, M. (1982) *Special Education and Social Control: Invisible Disasters* (London: Routledge & Kegan Paul)

FRANCIS, M. (1980a) 'Disruptive units: labelling a new generation', *Where*, April 1980

FRANCIS, M. (1980b) Letter to *The Times Education Supplement*, 5 December 1980

FRIERE, P. (1972) *Pedagogy of the Oppressed* (Harmondsworth: Penguin)

FURLONG, J. & BIRD, C. (1981) 'How Can We Cope With Karen?' *New Society*, 2 April 1981

GALLOWAY, D., BALL, T., BLOMFIELD, D. & SEYD, R. (1982) *Schools and Disruptive Pupils* (London: Longman)

GALWEY, J. (1979) 'What pupils think of special units', *Comprehensive Education*, no. 39, Winter 1979

GARFINKEL, H. (1956) 'Conditions of successful degradation ceremonies', *American Journal of Sociology*, no. 61

GOFFMAN, E. (1961) *Asylums* (New York: Doubleday)

GOFFMAN, E. (1963) *Stigma: Notes on the Management of Spoiled Identity* (Harmondsworth: Penguin)

GOLBY, M. (1978) *Institutional Alternatives*, Unit 15 in OU Course E363 (Milton Keynes: Open University Press)

GOLBY, M. (1979) 'Special Units: Some Educational Issues', *Socialism and Education* vol. 6, no. 2

GRUNSELL, R. (1978) *Born to be Invisible* (London: Macmillan)

GRUNSELL, R. (1980a) *Absent from School* (London: Writers & Readers)

GRUNSELL, R. (1980b) *Beyond Control?* (London: Writers & Readers)

HALSEY, A. H. *et al.* (1980) *Origins and Destinations* (Oxford: OUP)

HAMBLIN, D. H. (1974) *The Teacher and Counselling* (Oxford: Basil Blackwell)

HAMMERSLEY, M. & WOODS, P. (eds) (1976) *The Process of Schooling* (London: Routledge & Kegan Paul)

HARGREAVES, D. H. (1967) *Social Relations in a Secondary School* (London: Routledge & Kegan Paul)

HARGREAVES, D. H. (1972) *Interpersonal Relations and Education* (London: Routledge & Kegan Paul)

HARGREAVES, D. H., HESTOR, S. K. & MELLOR, F. J. (1975) *Deviance in Classrooms* (London: Routledge & Kegan Paul)

HARGREAVES, D. (1976) In Rutter, M. & Madge, N. (1976) q.v.

HARGREAVES, D. (1978) 'The two curricula and the community', *Westminster Studies in Education*, vol. 1

HART SHEA, T. & ROWLANDS, C. (1980) 'Play in the lunch hour', *ILEA Contact*, vol. 9, no. 19

HEAD, D. (ed.) (1974) *Free Way to Learning* (Harmondsworth: Penguin)

HILL, T. (1979) 'Disruption and Response', *Socialism and Education*, vol. 6, no. 2

HOLMAN, P. & LIBRETTO, G. (1979) 'The On-Site Unit', *Comprehensive Education*, no. 39, Winter 1979

HOME OFFICE (1981) *The Brixton Disorders* (the Scarman Report) (London: HMSO)

HUNKIN, J. & ALHADEFF, G. (1978) 'Therapeutic Education in Comprehensive Schools' (3), unpublished paper, Ilfracombe School and Community College

ILEA (1980) 'Support Centres Programme Monitoring Study: First Annual Report' (London: Inner London Education Authority)

ILEA (1981) 'Ethnic Census of School Support Centres and Educational Guidance Centres' (London: Inner London Education Authority)

JOHNSON, D., RANSOM, E., PACKWOOD, T., BOWDEN, K. & KOGAN, M. (1980) *Secondary Schools and the Welfare Network* (London: Allen & Unwin)

JONES, N. J. (1971) 'The Brislington Project in Bristol', *Special Education*, vol. 60, no. 2

JONES, N. J. (1973) 'Special Adjustment Units in Comprehensive Schools I and II', *Therapeutic Education*, vol. 1, no. 2

JONES, N. J. (1977) 'Special Maladjustment Units in Comprehensive Schools', *Therapeutic Education*, vol. 5, no. 2

JONES, N. J. & DAVIES, D. (1975) 'Special Adjustment Units in Comprehensive Schools IV', *Therapeutic Education*, vol. 3, no. 1

JORDAN, J. (1974) 'The organisation of perspectives in teacher-pupil relations: an interactionist approach', unpublished M.Ed. thesis, University of Manchester

KAMIN, L. J. (1974) *The Science and Politics of IQ* (New York: John Wiley)

KEDDIE, N. (1971) 'Classroom Knowledge', in Young, M. F. D. (ed.) *Knowledge and Control* (London: Collier Macmillan)

LANE, D. (1978a) (1978b) *The Impossible Child*, vols 1 and 2 (London: ILEA)

LASLETT, R. (1977) *Educating Maladjusted Children* (London: Crosby Lockwood Staples)

LAWRENCE, J., STEAD, D. & YOUNG, P. E. (1978) *Disruptive Behaviour in a Secondary School* (London: Goldsmith's College)

LAWTON, D. (1980) *The Politics of the School Curriculum* (London: Routledge & Kegan Paul)

LEACH, D. J. & RAYBOULD, A. C. (1979) *Learning and Behaviour Difficulties in School* (London: Open Books)

LEMERT, E. (1951) *Social Pathology* (New York: McGraw-Hill)

LLOYD-SMITH, M. (1979) 'The Meaning of Special Units', *Socialism and Education*, vol. 6, no. 2

LING, R. (1982) 'Listening to NOISE: the strains of discord?', in *NOISE Journal*, 1982

LIVERPOOL EDUCATION COMMITTEE (1974) *The Suspended Child* (Liverpool Education Committee)

MACBEATH, J. (1977) 'Goodbye free school, hello special unit', *The Times Educational Supplement*, 9 December 1977

MARLAND, M. (1977) 'Talk to the Institute for the Study and Treatment of Delinquency', in *Psychology Today*, vol. 3, no. 4

MATZA, D. (1964) *Delinquency and Drift* (New York: Wiley)

MATZA, D. (1969) *Becoming Deviant* (Englewood Cliffs: Prentice Hall)

MAYS, J. (1973) 'Delinquent and Maladjusted Children', in Varma, V. P. (ed.) *Stresses in Children* (London: University of London Press)

MECHANIC, D. (1968) *Medical Sociology* (New York: Free Press)

MCMANUS, M. (1982) 'Raise Eyebrow not Fists', *The Times Educational Supplement*, 10 September 1982, no. 3454

MIDWINTER, E. (1977) 'Teaching with the urban environment', in Raynor, J. & Harris, E. (eds) (1977) *Schooling in the City* (London: Ward Lock)

MILLHAM, S. *et al.* (1976) 'On Violence in Community Houses', in Tutt, N. (ed.) (1976) *Violence* (London: HMSO)

MURGATROYD, S. (1980) *Helping the Troubled Child: Interprofessional Case Studies* (Harper & Row)

MUSGRAVE, P. W. (1975) 'The Place of Social Work in Schools', *Community Development Journal*, vol. 10, no. 1

NATIONAL ASSOCIATION OF SCHOOLMASTERS (1974) *Discipline in Schools* (Hemel Hempstead: NAS)

NATIONAL UNION OF TEACHERS (1976) *Discipline in Schools* (London: NUT)

NOISE (1982) Disaffected pupils – whose problem? Who cares?', *NOISE Journal*, Spring 1982

PEACEY, N. (1982) 'LEAP London Educational Alternatives Programme', in *NOISE Journal*, Spring 1982

POTTS, P. (1982a) *Biology and Handicap* (Milton Keynes: Open University Press)

POTTS, P. (1982b)   *The Professionals* (Milton Keynes: Open University Press)

POWER, M. *et al.* (1967)   'Delinquent schools?', *New Society*, 19 October 1967

POWER, M. *et al.* (1972)   'Neighbourhood schools and juveniles before the court', *British Journal of Criminology*, vol. 12, no. 3

PRINGLE, M. K. (1973)   *The Roots of Violence and Vandalism* (London: National Childrens Bureau)

PROFESSIONAL ASSOCIATION OF TEACHERS (1976)   *Discipline, Rewards and Punishments* (Derby: PAT)

PURKEY, W. W. (1970)   *Self Concept and School Achievement* (Englewood Cliffs, NJ: Prentice Hall)

RABINOWITZ, A. (1981)   'The Range of Solutions: A Critical Analysis', in Gillham, B. (ed.) (1981) *Problem Behaviour in the Secondary School* (London: Croom Helm)

REEVES, F. W. (1977)   'Alienation and Education', unpublished M.Ed. dissertation, University of Birmingham

REEVES, F. W. (1978)   'Alienation and the Secondary School Student', *Educational Review*, vol. 30, no. 2

REYNOLDS, D. (1976a)   'The Delinquent School', in Hammersley, M. & Woods, P. (eds) (1976) q.v.

REYNOLDS, D. (1976b)   'When Teachers and Pupils Refuse a Truce', in Mungham, G. and Pearson, G. (eds) (1976) *British Working Class Youth Culture* (London: Routledge & Kegan Paul)

REYNOLDS, D. & MURGATROYD, S. (1977)   'The Sociology of Schooling and the Absent Pupil: The School as a Factor in the Generation of Truancy', in Carroll, H. C. M. (ed.), *Absenteeism in South Wales: Studies of Pupils, their Homes and their Secondary School* (Swansea, University College)

REYNOLDS, D. (1978)   'Education and the Prevention of Delinquency', in Tull, N. S. (ed.) (1978), *Alternative Strategies of Coping with Crime* (Oxford: Basil Blackwell)

RICHARDSON, A. J. (1983)   'Approaches to Problematic Pupil Behaviour: a Sociological Study', unpublished M.A. thesis, University of Warwick

ROSE, G. & MARSHALL, T. F. (1974)   *Counselling and School Social Work* (New York: Wiley)

ROSSER, E. & HARRE, R. (1976)   'The meaning of "trouble",' in Hammersley, M. & Woods, P. (eds) (1976) q.v.

RUST, V. (1977)   *Alternatives in Education* (London: Sage Publications)

RUTTER, M. & MADGE, N. (1976)   *Cycles of Disadvantage* (London: Heinemann)

RUTTER, M. *et al.* (1979)   *Fifteen Thousand Hours: Secondary Schools and their Effects on Children* (London: Open Books)

SCHRAG, P. & DIVOKY, D. (1981)   *The Myth of the Hyperactive*

Child and Other Means of Child Control (Harmondsworth: Penguin)

SCHUTZ, A. (1944) 'The Stranger', *American Journal of Sociology*, vol. 49, no. 6

SCHUTZ, A. (1972) *The Phenomenology of the Social World* (London: Heinemann)

SCHUTZ, A. (1973) *The Structures of the Life-World* (London: Heinemann)

SCOTT, R. A. & DOUGLAS, J. D. (1972) *Theoretical Perspectives on Deviance* (New York: Basic Books)

SCOTTISH EDUCATION DEPARTMENT (1977) *Truancy and Indiscipline in Scottish Schools* (The Pack Report) (Glasgow: Scottish Education Department)

SEARLE, C. (1973) *This New Season* (London: Calder & Boyars)

SEAVER, N. B. (1973) 'The effects of naturally induced teacher expectations', *Journal of Personality and Social Psychology*, vol. 28, no. 3

SIMON, B. (1971) *Intelligence, Psychology and Education: A Marxist Critique* (London: Lawrence & Wishart)

STAFFORDSHIRE EDUCATION COMMITTEE (1977) *Disruptive Pupils in Schools* (Stafford: Staffordshire Education Committee)

SWAILES, A. (1979) 'Experiment at Parkhead Centre', *Special Education – Forward Trends*, vol. 6, no. 1

SWANN, W. (ed.) (1981) *The Practice of Special Education* (Oxford: Basil Blackwell)

SWANN, W. (1982) *Psychology and Special Education* (Milton Keynes: Open University Press)

TATTUM, D. (1982) *Disruptive Pupils in Schools and Units* (Chichester: John Wiley)

TAYLOR, M., MILLER, J. & OLIVEIRA, M. (1979) 'The project', *Comprehensive Education*, no. 39, winter 1979

THOMAS, D. & SWANN, W. (1982) *Family Views* (Milton Keynes: Open University Press)

THORNBURY, R. (1978) *The Changing Urban School* (London: Methuen)

TIMES EDUCATIONAL SUPPLEMENT (1980) ' "Sin bins" a big success', 14 November 1980

TOMLINSON, S. (1981) *Educational Subnormality – A Study in Decision Making* (London: Routledge & Kegan Paul)

TOMLINSON, S. (1982) *A Sociology of Special Education* (London: Routledge & Kegan Paul)

TOPPING, K. J. (1983) *Educational Systems for Disruptive Adolescents* (London: Croom Helm)

TOPPING, K. J. & QUELCH, T. (1976) *Special Units and Classes for Children with Behaviour Problems* (Calderdale: Metropolitan Borough of Calderdale, Psychology Service)

WALTERS, J. A. (1977)   *Sent Away: A Study of Young Offenders in Care* (Farnborough: Saxon House)

WASP, D. (1980)   'A course in integrated studies', *Special Education – Forward Trends*, vol. 7, no. 1

WERTHMAN, C. (1963)   'Delinquents in School: A test for the Legitimacy of Authority', Cosin, B. R. *et al.* (eds) (1971) *School and Society* (London: Routledge & Kegan Paul/Open University)

WEST, D. J. & FARRINGDON, D. (1973)   *Who becomes Delinquent?* (London: Heinemann)

WHITE, R. (1979)   'The ROSLA Project', *Socialism and Education*, vol. 6, no. 2

WHITE, R. (1980)   *Absent with Cause* (London: Routledge & Kegan Paul)

WHITE, R. & BROCKINGTON, D. (1978)   *In and Out of School* (London: Routledge & Kegan Paul)

WHITE LION STREET FREE SCHOOL (1979)   'A free school "curriculum"', in Whitty, G. & Young, M. (eds) (1976)   *Explorations in the Politics of School Knowledge* (Driffield: Nafferton Books)

WILLIS, P. (1977)   *Learning to Labour* (Farnborough: Saxon House)

WILSON, M. & EVANS, M. (1980)   *The Education of Disturbed Pupils* (London: Schools Council/Evans)

WOODS, P. (1976)   'Having a Laugh: an Antidote to Schooling', in Hammersley, M. & Woods, P. (eds) (1976) q.v.

YOUNG, P., STEED, D. & LAWRENCE, J. (1980)   'Local education authorities and autonomous off-site units for disruptive pupils in secondary schools', *Cambridge Journal of Education*, vol. 10, no. 2

Index of names

Index of subjects